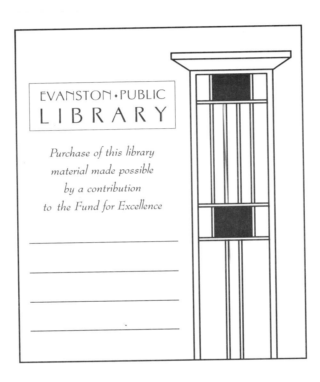

Thames & Hudson

HELENA ATTLEE

PHOTOGRAPHS BY ALEX RAMSAY

# The Most Beautiful
# Country Towns
# of Provence

*With 260 color illustrations*

Half title page
*This quiet side street leads off one of the main boulevards of
Saint-Rémy-de-Provence (Bouches-du-Rhône).*

Title pages
*The campanile of the basilica of Saint-Michel rises against the
background of the Mediterranean at Menton (Alpes-Maritimes).*

These pages
*Sunset heightens the warm tones of Saint-Paul-de-Vence
(Alpes-Maritimes).*

© 2002 Thames & Hudson Ltd, London
Text © 2002 Helena Attlee
Photographs © 2002 Alex Ramsay

First published in hardcover in the United States of America in 2002
by Thames & Hudson Inc., 500 Fifth Avenue, New York,
New York 10110

thamesandhudsonusa.com

Library of Congress Catalog Card Number 2001099695
ISBN 0-500-51087-3

Printed and bound in Singapore by C. S. Graphics

# Contents

# Introduction

Whatever your definition of Provence – and its exact boundaries are often disputed – it is a very special land of extraordinary variety and great beauty. It encompasses dramatic alpine scenery, fierce, rock-strewn plateaux, impossibly deep gorges, mellow pasture-land, vineyards, olive groves, salt marshes and the coastal strip with its lush, Mediterranean vegetation. Bathed in miraculously clear light, this is the landscape that has inspired brilliance in writers and artists for centuries.

Travellers have always commented on the distinct character of Provence. They compare it to Spain, to Italy, but never to the rest of France. The region's unique identity is distilled from a cocktail of foreign influences that have built up, layer upon layer, over the centuries. Greeks, Romans, Celts, Ligurians, Teutons and Moors all occupied Provence during the first three thousand years of its recorded history. It is said that we have the Ancient Greeks to thank for the olive trees that are integral to the landscape, and thus for the oil used so abundantly in Provençal cooking. The legacy of the Roman occupation is largely architectural. It is certainly true that Provence has some of the finest Roman remains anywhere outside Italy: the mausoleum and triumphal arch close to Saint-Rémy-de-Provence, the amphitheatre in Arles and the magnificent aqueduct between Uzès and Nîmes.

The country towns portrayed so vividly in Alex Ramsay's photographs are fiercely individual, displaying a great range of different architectural styles that reflect Provence's fragmented political history, and the extremes of its climate and geography. In Barcelonnette, for example, an alpine town in the far north of the region, the houses are built to withstand harsh winter weather. Their generous, overshot roofs are steeply pitched to shed the snow that often falls as early as October. If you were to leave Barcelonnette and travel eastwards, to Sospel or Menton perhaps, you would be just as likely to think yourself in Italy as in France. The Italianate influence that was first exerted by the Romans has run unbroken through the politics and culture of Provence. It is this influence that we see

*D*ramatic landscapes and the observance of traditional customs are the very stuff of life in Provence. The curious shadow at sunset on the corrugated face of Sisteron's Rocher de la Baume (opposite) *is that of the town's gigantic citadel. In Saint-Rémy-de-Provence* (above) *thousands of sheep are driven through the town at Pentecôte to mark the beginning of their transfer to alpine pastures.*

*M*arkets, venerable buildings and stunning scenery lend the towns of Provence their unique character: baskets for sale in Villeneuve-lès-Avignon (left); St. John's cloister at the heart of Villeneuve-lès-Avignon's magnificent charterhouse (below).

reflected in the Baroque churches and ochre-coloured houses of the Alpes-Maritimes. Once within the *comté* of Nice, these towns were under the control of Italian Savoy for almost 500 years.

Italy's influence was by no means restricted to the eastern part of the region. In 1274 the papacy claimed the area of the Vaucluse then known as the Comtat Venaissin. Later, Avignon became the seat of the magnificent papal court, a focus for all that was finest in Italian culture. Although the Pope returned to Rome in 1376, taking his entourage of artists, writers and musicians with him, the Comtat was not restored to France until the Revolution, remaining a separate country within Provence until then, with its own border posts and passports. Its residents were immune from French law, a fact that attracted criminals and minority groups.

*Natural and man-made drama in northern Provence: Sisteron's citadel rises from the early morning mist* (above).

*M*oustiers faïence *jars provide a decorative note in the eighteenth-century pharmacy of the Hôtel-Dieu, still the main hospital in Carpentras. In cabinets* (above) *there are carefully labelled bottles which contain an exotic mixture of remedies, such as dragon's blood and cantharides ('Spanish fly').*

It was medieval Provence that caught the imagination of the poet Frédéric Mistral (1830–1914). With a number of other writers and artists, he formed a group called the Félibrige. Together, they created a romantic mythology around the Counts of Provence, their austere castles, and the courts where troubadours sang songs or recited poems written in the beautiful *langue d'oc*. Mistral, who was always the best-known of the group, was awarded the Nobel Prize in 1901. His statue, unmistakable in its wide-awake hat, stands in the main square of almost every town in Provence, reflecting the status he achieved by reminding the Provençal people of their identity and teaching them to be proud of their language and traditions.

Provence has also been championed by other writers, notably Alphonse Daudet, born in Nîmes, Marcel Pagnol from Aubagne near Marseilles and Jean Giono, a native of the Lubéron. Each of them evokes a powerful yet different image. But, then, Provence invites invention, with its multi-faceted landscape and the many layers of its cultural history. The region also acted as a magnet for a dazzling array of foreign writers. Somerset Maugham, D. H. Lawrence, Virginia Woolf and Scott Fitzgerald were all drawn to Provence between the two World Wars.

To painters, Provence offers a quality of light that can be found nowhere else in the world. Although miraculous in its clarity, it is changeable, quite lacking the brassy consistency of the conditions found elsewhere in the Mediterranean. This must be due in part to the Mistral, a savage wind that tears down the Rhône valley whenever there is a depression over the sea. From the end of the nineteenth century a number of distinguished artists, inspired by the work of Van Gogh and Cézanne, began to find their way to Provence. The list of names associated with the towns of the coast and the countryside inland reads like a catalogue of the finest art of the early twentieth century: Picasso, Monet, Renoir, Signac, Matisse, Dufy, Bonnard, Léger, Chagall. Much of that beauty of place which inspired them is caught in the photographs which illustrate this book.

# GARD & BOUCHES-DU-RHÔNE

*The Rhône valley forms the frontier between Provence and the rest of France. The dazzling, limpid quality of the light is apparent as soon as you cross the border from the Ardèche. This is the historic heart of Provence, the site of some of the greatest Roman monuments outside Italy. Arles, at the mouth of the Rhône delta, was capital of Roman Gaul. The area is also associated with the medieval troubadours, the lyric poets who led the development of vernacular poetry and idolized romantic love in a crude and violent age.*

*Both Gard and Bouches-du-Rhône veered towards Protestantism, a position that cost them dear during the Wars of Religion, when Uzès lost its cathedral. After the Edict of Nantes was revoked in 1685, re-establishing Catholicism as the sole authorized religion, many of the Huguenot inhabitants of the area emigrated to South Africa, America and the Protestant countries of Europe.*

*The bell-tower of the collegiate church of Notre-Dame in Villeneuve-lès-Avignon was originally built over an arcade of four pillars that straddled the public road. Nearly twenty years after it was built, the chapter obtained royal permission to wall in the arcades, thus creating a choir for the church.*

# *Aigues-Mortes*

GARD

AIGUES-MORTES is best seen from a spit of land bordering the great expanse of the Étang de la Ville to the south of the town. There, gaudy pink flamingos stand about in dark blue water; beyond, defensive ramparts rise like gigantic cardboard cut-outs from reed beds, dominated by the overblown cylinder of the Tour de Constance, standing behind a cluster of jostling masts.

When Louis IX, or St. Louis, commissioned the construction of the tower in 1241, he was taking the first step in the realization of a great plan. The desolate stretch of marshland that he had managed to buy from a local monastery was of little agricultural value, but it had enormous strategic importance. It represented the opportunity for Louis to become the first French king with a port on the Mediterranean, giving France access for the first time to the rich trade with Italy and the Orient. It was also a foothold in the south, right on the border of territory belonging to the Holy Roman Empire.

At the time, St. Louis' tower was probably the largest structure to have been built in Provence since the fall of the Roman Empire. But for the arrow slits that pierce its monolithic walls, the smooth yellow exterior is unbroken. A lighthouse turret is the only addition to the perfectly cylindrical form. The entrance, which was equipped with a portcullis, can be

*S**een here across the Chenal Maritime, the Tour de Constance served over the centuries as a fortress, lighthouse, look-out post and prison* (left).
*This thirteenth-century image of a boat* (above) *is carved on the reveal of a window inside the tower.*

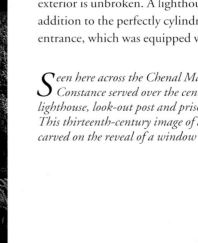

reached only by means of a narrow bridge across the moat. Inside, the building is surprisingly beautiful. The circular guard room on the ground floor has a handsome fireplace and a vaulted ceiling. It is overlooked by a first-floor gallery, from which archers could shoot at any intruder who had penetrated the outer defences. Another large room on the second floor was used for hundreds of years as a prison. Many of the inmates were prisoners of conscience, incarcerated for their religious or political beliefs. After the Edict of Nantes was revoked in 1685, all of the town's towers were used as prisons for Huguenots who refused to convert to Catholicism. From 1715 the tower was used exclusively for women. Rough, spindly letters that spell the word *register* ('resist' in the dialect of the Ardèche) are said to have been carved in

*Massive ramparts rise beside the Porte de la Gardette (left); another gate, the Porte des Moulins, leads into the Rue Théaulon on the southern edge of the town (below left). In the centre lies animated Place Saint-Louis (below) amid streets best viewed from the Tour de Constance (opposite).*

the floor by Marie Durand, a young woman committed in 1730, and famous for her courage and leadership of the other women.

In St. Louis' lifetime Aigues-Mortes consisted of the solitary Tour de Constance and a small town, constructed mostly in wood. It stood right at the edge of a lake which served as the inner harbour, linked by two channels to the outer harbour and the open sea. A causeway had to be built through the marshes to join the new town to terra firma. Although the tower was a magnificent symbol of Capetian power in that far-flung place, it did nothing to make the stagnant lakes and marshland of Aigues-Mortes an attractive place to live. The King had to tempt inhabitants to the new town by offering incentives such as tax exemptions.

What really brought the place to life was the Pope's decision to ask St. Louis to lead the Seventh Crusade to the Holy Land, using Aigues-Mortes as the embarkation point. When the Crusade finally departed on 28 August 1248, preparations had been under way for four years. Vast quantities of wheat, barley and wine had already been shipped from the new harbour to Cyprus, the first destination. Days before the final departure, a fleet of 1,500 ships, chartered from Marseilles, Genoa and Venice, assembled in the port. More food was loaded, along with weapons and horses. Knights from all over France must have descended on the little town, demanding stabling and buying last-minute provisions.

Although Aigues-Mortes was to see the launch of another crusade in 1270, no further work was done by Louis to the town's fortifications. It was Philip III who finally commissioned the mighty encircling wall and ramparts, and Philip IV who completed them. The entire fortification complex was built in less than forty years, making Aigues-Mortes a perfectly preserved example of cutting-edge military architecture at the end of the thirteenth century.

*T*he wild ponies of the Camargue (above) graze the salt marshes near the town; beyond the Étang de la Marette (right) rise ramparts and towers.

# *Arles*

BOUCHES-DU-RHÔNE

AWAY FROM THE BUSY BOULEVARD DES LICES, Arles is a gentle, engaging town. In summer it draws crowds of tourists, but in autumn and winter, when the Mistral whistles down the Rhône valley, the streets are almost empty.

The gargantuan, scarred walls of the Roman amphitheatre dominate the skyline of the old town, dwarfing the houses around it. Built in the latter part of the first century A.D., it could seat an audience of 20,000 for the gruesome spectacles held there. Its magnificent size reflects the glorious period when, as Arelate, Arles was the most important Roman city beyond the Alps, serving as capital not only for Rome's first 'province' outside Italy, but for the whole of Gaul, Spain and England as well.

It is not difficult to understand why the medieval population of the town should have treated their amphitheatre as a ready-made fortress in times of trouble. After the fall of the Roman Empire, the Normans and the Saracens made repeated attacks on the town. At first the citizens simply barricaded

*The façade of the Musée Réattu (left) was once part of the medieval town walls. Later, it became a priory, and then a private house belonging to the painter Jacques Réattu (1760–1833). A familiar sight in the towns of Provence, Frédéric Mistral's statue stands in the Place du Forum (above).*

21

themselves inside the huge, encircling walls. They had no reason to respect the ancient structure that gave them shelter, and soon they began to pick away at it, using the stone to build houses. Over the years, the amphitheatre turned into a small walled town within Arles. The arcades, the galleries, the tiers and the arena itself were slowly filled by some two hundred houses and two chapels. Although their houses were built of stone, the inhabitants of the amphitheatre had no running water or sewers. In these conditions, it is not surprising that a plague in 1721 claimed a large number of victims. It was not until the beginning of the nineteenth century that the site was eventually cleared to reveal the building's original form.

Another great Roman legacy is the hauntingly beautiful graveyard, Les Alyscamps, outside the town walls. It is a wonderful legacy of the period when Christianity was gradually gathering force in Provence. The thick-set, weather-beaten Roman sarcophagi

*The twelfth-century bell-tower of Saint-Trophime* (opposite) *was completed just before the magnificent portal* (below), *built in a form reminiscent of a Roman triumphal arch. On one side of the portal Satan presides over a figure representing concupiscence* (right).

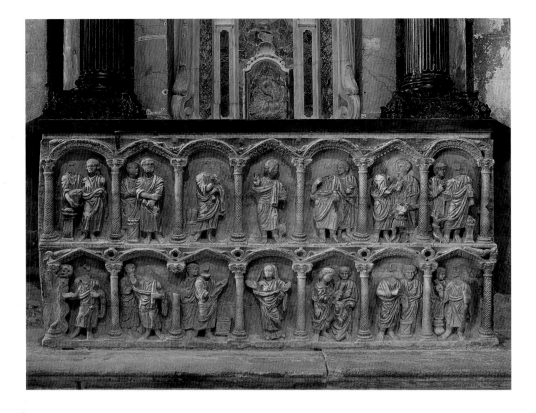

stand on either side of a road that leads to the church of Saint-Honorat. This was originally a Romanesque chapel, then rebuilt in the twelfth century. Lit only by a two-storey lantern in its domed ceiling, on sunny days the church is transformed into a box of light. The sarcophagi that occupy the side chapels are much better preserved than the ones outside. There is one particularly impressive sarcophagus, dating from the third century, that is decorated with tragic masks on the hipped corners of its lid.

When the finishing touches were put to Saint-Trophime in 1178, it was considered one of the most important cathedrals in Europe. Almost at once, it was used for the coronation of the Holy Roman Emperor, Frederick Barbarossa. The cathedral façade has recently been cleaned, revealing the full glory of the detailed carving on the portal. Christ occupies the tympanum, and on the frieze below him the saved queue up quietly on the left of the door, flanked by angels. To the right the damned, naked and chained, are ushered along by a demon. Around the corner they meet their doom in the flames of hell. Below this vivid scene are life-size figures of saints.

*Saint-Trophime contains many treasures, including the fourth-century tomb of St. Honoratus (above left), which was used for many years as the high altar in the chapel dedicated to the saint at Les Alycamps (left); the lives of the apostles are depicted in two tiers of elaborate carving. The Adoration of the Magi (above) by Louis Finsonius (1580–1617), dated 1614, hangs in the Chapelle des Rois (opposite).*

*T*he High Baroque altarpiece and retable (opposite) *dominates the Chapelle des Jesuites in the Rue Balze. Beneath the chapel lies a complex of underground galleries and chambers* (above right), *originally part of the Roman forum; their exact use has never been determined, although after the Romans left Provence the well-ventilated corridors were used as granaries. A memorial to Amédée Pichot* (above left) *stands on the street of the same name just inside the Porte de la Cavalerie; Pichot (1795–1877) translated many of the classics of English literature into French. The famous Roman cemetery of Arles, Les Alyscamps* (left), *is laid out along the route of the Via Aurelia to Rome.*

*R*oman rule left an indelible mark on Arles; the theatre (below) was built during the rule of Augustus, and is a century older than the amphitheatre (right). Both sites are still in regular use.

The cathedral chapter did not raise the money for the cloister of Saint-Trophime until the end of the twelfth century. The north and east galleries were the first to be built. The capitals of the delicate, double pilasters are carved on the inside with evocative scenes from the life and passion of Christ. On one the Massacre of the Innocents is shown, the soldiers wearing chain-mail and dangling the poor babies by their hair. Between the columns are bas-reliefs of the saints, their clothing carved with precise and delicate detail, down to the decorative trims on collars and cuffs. Work on the cloister was interrupted when the cathedral chapter had to raise funds, first for a crusade and then for the ransoms demanded by the Saracens for the release of prisoners. It was not until the fourteenth century that money could be raised for the completion of the cloister. The south and west sections were built in the slightly less elaborate style of the Gothic period, but the two parts sit together in surprising harmony in a silence broken only by the conversations of pigeons and the cacophony of bells on the hour.

# Saint-Rémy-de-Provence

BOUCHES-DU-RHÔNE

BUILT BENEATH THE ALPILLES RANGE – miniature mountains as fantastic as any in a child's drawing – lies Saint-Rémy. The fields around the town are planted with soft fruit, vegetables and cutting flowers. Around each field is a barricade of sturdy cypresses, poplars or even bamboo lashed together to form a fence. When the Mistral comes screaming through, it is easy to understand the purpose of these preparations.

Saint-Rémy-de-Provence is usually a peaceful place, its little squares submerged in the dappled shade cast by plane trees. At Pentecôte, however, the town is transformed by a lively crowd of local people and passing tourists that floods the streets to watch the Transhumance Festival. The movement of sheep and goats to summer pastures is of great importance in the *département* of Bouches-du-Rhône. Each summer a million sheep are sent off to the Alpine massif at the

*A view over the roofs of Saint-Rémy (left) reveals the elegant Gothic bell-tower of Saint-Martin against the backdrop of the Alpilles; erected in 1330, the tower was completely rebuilt in 1736. A Corinthian colonnade tops the Roman mausoleum just outside Saint-Rémy (above).*

31

end of June, where they will stay until mid October. During the festival a flock of about 3,000 is driven around the boulevards that enclose the old town, transforming it into a river of pale fleece punctuated only by small groups of chestnut-coloured goats with long, twisted horns. The sheep are merinos, a breed with pale eyelashes and distinctive, monkey-like faces.

The largest building in Saint-Rémy is the church of Saint-Martin, a huge Neoclassical structure with an interior modelled on that of St. Peter's in Rome. It was erected to replace a medieval church which collapsed one dramatic night in 1818. The Gothic bell-tower is the only survivor of the original structure. There are also some fine houses in Saint-Rémy. The Hôtel Mistral de Mondragon, for example, is a beautiful sixteenth-century building with a central courtyard

overlooked by loggias. Standing on the Place Favier, an intimate square lined with trees, it houses the local history museum. Around the corner is the Hôtel de Sade, a slightly earlier building, which is now an archaeological museum devoted to finds from the nearby Roman site of Glanum.

The most striking of the buildings associated with Glanum are to be found on the road outside Saint-Rémy. Built during the early years of Augustus' reign, shortly before the birth of Christ, the so-called mausoleum is an unforgettable sight. It was not a tomb, in fact, but a cenotaph built to commemorate a nobleman from Saint-Rémy and his wife. It is the sheer size of the structure and its extraordinary state of preservation that make it so striking. The roof of the rotunda at the top rises to 18 metres (60 feet). Delicate

*Saint-Rémy is a delightfully compact place, full of quiet corners, like the shady Place Favier (below). Pleasantly aged buildings contain history within their stones: the Hôtel de Sade (opposite) was once a priory and then served as the parish church.*

*A nineteenth-century fountain (opposite) commemorates the birth of Michel de Nostradame, named Nostradamus, in Saint-Rémy in 1503. A true Renaissance polymath, Nostradamus practised as a medical doctor, studied philosophy and analysed Egyptian hieroglyphics, as well as writing* The Centuries, *a book of enigmatic predictions first published in 1555. The fountain stands at the corner of Saint-Rémy's main street, the Rue Carnot (above). On the day of the Transhumance Festival (right), shepherds wearing traditional costume drive their flocks along the boulevards that encircle the town.*

*Among the most famous and best preserved Roman monuments in Europe, the triumphal arch and mausoleum (opposite above left) stand to the south of Saint-Rémy, where they once marked the entrance to Glanum (opposite below). Magnificent bas-reliefs (opposite above right) decorate the mausoleum. Simple fountains like this one at Mas de la Pyramide (right), a farm in Glanum owned and worked by the same family for centuries, have hardly changed since Roman times.*

carving decorates it at every level, and bas-reliefs depicting hunting and battle scenes adorn the four sides of the podium. Next to the mausoleum is the triumphal arch that once straddled the entrance to Glanum from the west. Another structure of perfect proportions, it is decorated with swags of leaves and fruit. The friezes on the sides show mournful prisoners.

Saint-Rémy has many other things to be proud of. In 1503 it saw the birth of Michel de Nostradamus, doctor turned astrologer, upon whose predictions the famously superstitious Catherine de' Medici is said to

have relied. A nineteenth-century fountain to his memory stands on the corner of the Rue Nostradamus and the Rue Carnot. The town was also home to the poet Joseph Roumanille. Born in 1818, he was one of the founder members of the Félibrige, the group of poets and writers who worked to revive the customs of old Provence and the language of the troubadours, reduced over the centuries to little more than crude slang. It is said that he reached the decision to write in Provençal long before the founding of the Félibrige in 1854. Roumanille began his career by writing poems in French, but one day, while reading his work aloud to a

group of friends, he noticed his mother weeping. Provençal was her first language, and she explained that she could not speak French well enough to understand his verse. That was a turning-point for Roumanille, or so the story goes, and the start of a life-long campaign to champion his native tongue. He was by no means alone in this aim. Victor Gélu (1806–85), the revolutionary poet from Marseilles, and Jacques Boé (1798–1864) had declared similar intentions. Frédéric Mistral, Nobel Laureate in 1901 and by far the most famous member of the movement, lived in the neighbouring village of Maillane.

The famous association of Saint-Rémy and Van Gogh was not a happy one. Between the spring of 1889 and that of 1890, the artist lived in the local lunatic asylum of Saint-Paul-de-Mausole. His output during that brief period was astonishing. He painted 150 canvases, often working outside, in the garden and the surrounding countryside, where narrow paths quarter the fields surrounding the asylum walls. At first these look like sheep or goat tracks, but in fact they have been worn by the feet of generations of visitors in search of the exact views immortalized by Van Gogh.

*The short period Van Gogh spent in the asylum of Saint-Paul-de-Mausole (above) proved to be one of the most productive of his life. Although there is still a hospital on the site, the pretty cloister (left), his room and the church are open to visitors.*

Overleaf
*Local inhabitants pause to chat outside the local history museum, the Musée des Alpilles, on the Place Favier (p. 40). Beyond the square, the cobbled Rue du Parage runs beneath a fifteenth-century archway (p. 41).*

HÔTEL DE MISTRAL
DE MONTDRAGON
XVIᵉ SIÈCLE

# Tarascon &
# Beaucaire

BOUCHES-DU-RHÔNE & GARD

AS YOU CROSS THE RHÔNE FROM BEAUCAIRE, the sheer
size of Tarascon's castle seems shocking. Its pale
smooth walls rise out of rough, unworked rock, their
reflection shimmering on the dark waters of the river. A
castle has stood at this strategic point on the banks of
the Rhône ever since the Romans occupied Provence.
Louis II of Anjou began to rebuild his ancestor's rough,
thirteenth-century fortress in 1400. The new building
defined Provence's western boundary, looking across
the Rhône to Beaucaire in the kingdom of France. By
1406 Louis had spent 34,000 florins on the fortified
walls and towers. After his death, work continued
under Louis III, who commissioned Jean Robert, a
master mason and one of Provence's finest architects,
to build the castle's main courtyard and the south and
east wings. (Continued on p.49)

*T*he colossal bulk of Tarascon's château (left) towers
above the Rhône; more modest fifteenth-century
houses (above) grace the pretty, arcaded Rue des Halles in
the centre of the town.

The elegant Gothic steeple of Tarascon's Sainte-Marthe (opposite) *was added to the church's Romanesque belfry in 1470; destroyed during the Second World War, it was restored in 1975. Local legend attributes the taming of the Tarasque monster (far left), depicted here in a bas-relief in the Hôtel de Ville, to St. Martha. Despite extensive wartime bombing, Tarascon has retained much of its town wall. This detail (left) is above the gate on the Rue Raspail. The beautiful Romanesque Chapelle Saint-Gabriel (below) stands in an olive grove on the Fontvieille road, just outside Tarascon.*

Overleaf
*Tarascon's Hôtel de Ville (p.46) boasts an impressive entrance from the market-place. In the Souleïado museum (p.47) are displayed the pigments and printing blocks used in making the firm's famous fabrics.*

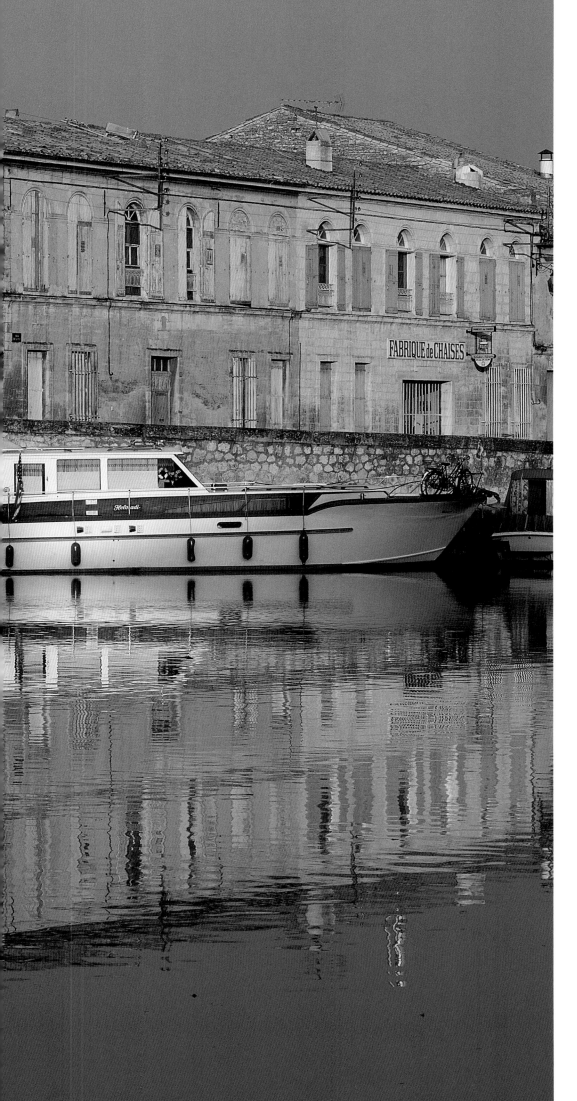

Louis III was succeeded by his brother, Good King René, a civilized Renaissance prince who was the last real sovereign of an independent Provence. When René came to power he was the titular King of Naples and Sicily, as well as Duke of Anjou and Count of Provence. His reign was not a political success. He spent six years of it in captivity after an unsuccessful territorial battle against the Duke of Burgundy. Shortly after paying a ransom for his own freedom, René lost the Kingdom of Naples to Alphonse V of Aragon. One military defeat followed another, and eventually René withdrew to Provence. He turned his back on political life and surrounded himself with artists and scholars, becoming a dedicated patron and author, poet and musician in his own right.

René completed Tarascon, turning the interior into a magnificent Renaissance palace, filled with painting, sculptures, tapestries and fine furniture. From the outside, the castle was still a forbidding place, a bellicose statement on the political frontier between one kingdom and another. Inside, the castle still creates a very different impression. The tone is set by the delicate and decorative courtyard at the heart of the building. Although as deep as a well-shaft, it is an uplifting space, overlooked by the large mullion windows that light the royal apartments. The state-rooms are all built in finely worked, pale limestone. Many of them have wooden, coffered ceilings exquisitely decorated with patterns of leaves and flowers. (Continued on p.54)

*T he southern limits of Beaucaire are marked by the Canal du Rhône* (left); *the belfry of Saint-Paul* (above) *is one of many architectural treasures in the town.*

Overleaf
*A number of fine seventeenth-century buildings line the streets of the town: the Hôtel de Fermineau* (p.50) *was once an Ursuline convent; the Hôtel de Margailler* (p.51) *has an entrance flanked by magnificent telamones.*

After King René's death in 1480, Tarascon castle fell gradually into dereliction. It became a prison, and in one room the seventeenth-century graffiti of English and Welsh sailors are still clearly visible. Detailed pictures of galleys, crudely coloured, are carved into the stone walls. When the castle eventually came into the hands of the State in 1840 it was severely run-down. In 1926 restoration work began. All additions to the original building were demolished, paring it down to the compact structure that we see today.

Despite suffering extensive damage during the Second World War, the centre of Tarascon is still very pleasant. The cobbled, arcaded streets fan out from the Hôtel de Ville, a striking building with a seventeenth-century façade. Closer to the castle is the church of Sainte-Marthe. It is said that the saint liberated Tarascon from the Tarasque, a terrible, amphibious monster that used to crawl out of the river and devour the inhabitants of the town. Her church became a place of pilgrimage and had to be enlarged so often that the original, Romanesque building is unrecognizable today.

Tarascon is also the home of the firm of Souleïado, manufacturers of the vibrant, printed cotton fabrics which are sold all over Provence. Their designs were originally inspired by printed cottons imported from the East Indies via Marseilles in the seventeenth century. In the Musée Souleïado there is a magnificent archive of the fruitwood blocks originally used for printing the fabrics.

The great architectural statement that is Tarascon did not go unanswered. Across the expanse of the Rhône is the French castle of Beaucaire. Although it was largely demolished on the orders of Cardinal Richelieu in 1632, Beaucaire still makes an imposing impression. The land between the castle and the river

*E*arly morning sunlight fills the Rue du 4 Septembre (below) *in the heart of Beaucaire; at about the same time the cafés and bars of the town* (opposite) *start to open.*

was once the site of the most important fair in Europe. First held in 1217 under Raymond VI of Toulouse, its popularity continued until the nineteenth century, when the railways finally undermined the Rhône's great importance as a trade route. Now the land is used only for picnics, bullfights and grazing by wintering circuses. The town still has a very businesslike atmosphere, but is pretty in an unselfconscious way which has nothing to do with tourism.

*The collegiate church of Notre-Dame-des-Pommiers* (left *and* below) *was transformed into a 'temple of reason' during the Revolution; originally a medieval structure, it was rebuilt between 1734 and 1744, because it had become too small to accommodate the congregation during Beaucaire's fair. The belfry of the church* (opposite) *is visible from the gardens below the château.*

# Uzès

GARD

BUILT FROM STONE THE COLOUR OF PALE HONEY, Uzès
is a handsome, tranquil town, its skylines adorned by
towers, battlements and belfries that create an
atmosphere of high romance. The ducal family of de
Crussol has lived in the heart of the old town for the
last millennium. The square keep of their eleventh-
century castle looms over the heavy medieval walls that
surround the palace of 1550. The forbidding effect of
the walls is rather undermined by an elegant gateway,
built during the sixteenth century. Beyond it lies an
intimate courtyard, its walls partially clad by a Virginia
creeper that burns red against the pale stone each
autumn.

The château is encircled by towers. Rising from the
far wall of the courtyard is the Tour de la Vicomté. A
delicate, octagonal structure that adds its own
statement to the unique skyline of Uzès, it was built to

*A general view of the town* (right) *reveals a
magnificent array of belfries and towers, including
the twelfth-century Tour Fenestrelle* (above); *the two top
storeys of the original structure were lost during the
Wars of Religion.*

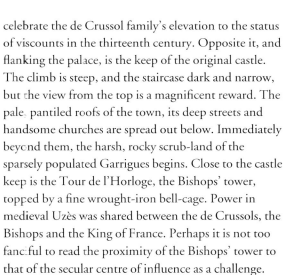

*A new façade was added to the cathedral of Saint-Théodorit (opposite) in the nineteenth century. This figure (left) decorates the seventeenth-century Bishop's Palace, which now houses a public library and a museum with a fine collection of local ceramics. The Pavillon Racine (below) once formed part of the town's fortifications; restored in the eighteenth century, it was named to commemorate the period that the playwright spent in Uzès with his uncle.*

different effects: the architectural version of a needlework sampler. Delorme, who had studied for three years in Rome, chose this moment to experiment by using all three classical orders in one design. The pillars, different on each of the building's three storeys, flank richly carved bas-relief panels.

By the fifth century Uzès was a bishopric. The original cathedral suffered at the hands of the Cathars during the Albigensian Wars. It was then completely destroyed in 1621, at the beginning of the Wars of Religion. Uzès had embraced Calvinism from the start, becoming Protestant in 1540 and soon developing into a Huguenot stronghold, a fact that led directly to the loss of its cathedral. All that remains of the original building is the Tour Fenestrelle, a beautiful, six-tiered Lombard bell-tower with arched windows which makes an exotic addition to the architecture of Uzès.

The new cathedral dates from 1637, although its original façade was replaced in 1871. The money for the construction of the seventeenth-century building was raised through a tax imposed on the purchase of meat

celebrate the de Crussol family's elevation to the status of viscounts in the thirteenth century. Opposite it, and flanking the palace, is the keep of the original castle. The climb is steep, and the staircase dark and narrow, but the view from the top is a magnificent reward. The pale, pantiled roofs of the town, its deep streets and handsome churches are spread out below. Immediately beyond them, the harsh, rocky scrub-land of the sparsely populated Garrigues begins. Close to the castle keep is the Tour de l'Horloge, the Bishops' tower, topped by a fine wrought-iron bell-cage. Power in medieval Uzès was shared between the de Crussols, the Bishops and the King of France. Perhaps it is not too fanciful to read the proximity of the Bishops' tower to that of the secular centre of influence as a challenge.

The Bishops of Uzès were granted exceptional powers by the King, including the right to mint money in the town. The Hôtel des Monnaies can still be seen on the corner of the Rue Docteur-Blanchard. The Crussol motto, *Ferro non auro* ('By iron and not by gold'), might be interpreted as a back-handed reference to the bishops and their mint. The motto appears below the family crest above the entrance to the palace. It is flanked by lions, rampant and roaring. Built to plans by Philibert Delorme in 1550, the pretty façade of the palace is a light-hearted fusion of

*One representative of the ecclesiastical presence in Uzès is the eighteenth-century church of Saint-Étienne (left). Secular power is asserted unequivocally by the square Tour Bermonde, the eleventh-century keep of the ducal palace (opposite), which dominates this view; in front of it is the tower of the family chapel, with the colourful de Crussol coat of arms incorporated in its tiled roof. In the heart of the town the arcaded Place aux Herbes (below) is tranquil enough below its aged plane trees.*

by the inhabitants of Uzès and levied for eight years. The nave and apse are flanked by magnificent galleries on three storeys. At the first level these galleries are enclosed by elaborate, gilded, wrought-iron screens, and on the second by more substantial stone balustrades. The cathedral's greatest treasure is its seventeenth-century organ. The gilded organ pipes could be concealed by a folding screen during Lent. The screen's wooden panels are decorated with delicate patterns painted in dove-grey and gold. Fortunately, the organ survived the mass destruction and pillaging that took place in Uzès during the Revolution.

During the Middle Ages, the life of Uzès revolved around the Place aux Herbes, an enchanting, irregular square enclosed by low arcades and shaded by plane trees. Today, the square is the setting for a lively market each week, and is always filled with agreeable smells from the restaurants and bakeries under the arcades.

*Delicious local produce is sold at the market held in the Place aux Herbes each week* (above left *and* below right). *This inviting antique shop* (left) *stands on the Place de l'Évêché, close to the cathedral of Saint-Théodorit* (opposite).

# Villeneuve-lès-Avignon

GARD

STANDING ON THE WEST BANK OF THE RHÔNE, Villeneuve-lès-Avignon has always retained its own identity, and an atmosphere quite distinct from that of the frenetic city of Avignon on the opposite side of the river. Elegant buildings line the tranquil, sunny streets, and above the town, beneath the monolithic walls of the Fort Saint-André, the silence is broken only by the screams of diving swallows.

Named, somewhat prosaically, as 'new town near Avignon', Villeneuve was founded on 11 July 1292 by King Philippe le Bel of France. Its position, on the easternmost edge of his kingdom, was of great strategic importance. When Pope Clement VI made Avignon the centre of Catholic Christendom, the small and, if we are to believe Petrarch, somewhat squalid town of Avignon was filled to overflowing almost at once. It seems that the King of France made no objection when large numbers of cardinals chose to live in Villeneuve, turning it into a suburb of Avignon. Over

*The eighteenth-century Saint-Jean fountain* (above) *stands in the centre of the cloister of the same name in the town's charterhouse, behind which lies the Fort Saint-André* (left) *on the summit of Mont Andaon.*

the years, 115 palaces were built, bringing an unexpected magnificence to the narrow streets of the country town.

One of the largest residences in Villeneuve was owned by Cardinal Étienne Aubert. When Pope Clement VI died in 1352, the papal conclave initially chose the General of the Carthusian Order as his successor. Humility led him to decline the throne, and Étienne Aubert was elected in his place as Innocent VI. Aubert commemorated the General's act by donating his dwelling on the Val de Bénédiction and all of his land to the Carthusians.

The charterhouse incorporated the chapel of Cardinal Aubert's original dwelling and his banqueting hall, which became the monks' refectory. At first there were only twelve monks, but the order grew along with the building. Eventually, three separate cloisters were built, making this the largest Carthusian monastery in France. The charterhouse has not been inhabited since the Revolution, but it has been beautifully restored to give a wonderfully vivid impression of monastic life. The largest of the three cloisters, built in pale limestone and decorated by nothing more than alternate stripes of sun and shade, is lined by the small doors of innumerable cells. Behind them the rooms inhabited by the Carthusian fathers have been reconstructed. Each has a workshop, a bedroom and a small, walled garden where the scent of roses is reflected off the hot walls.

*T*he largest of the charterhouse's three cloisters, the Cloître du Cimetière (above) stands against the dramatic backdrop of the Fort Saint-André. The view from the fort (right) encompasses Avignon on the opposite bank of the Rhône; the towers of the Palais des Papes are clearly visible.

A small chapel lies at the far end of the cloister. Originally part of the Aubert residence , it is decorated with frescoes by Matteo Giovanetti, an Italian artist from Siena whose use of perspective was remarkable for the fourteenth century. The church is on the other side of the complex, a beautiful, severe building built in the sober southern Gothic style. The end of the apse collapsed in the nineteenth century and now the nave offers a marvellous view of Fort Saint-André on the hillside above. Pope Innocent VI's tomb, which lies in its own chapel on the north side of the apse, was elaborately carved from Pernes stone by Thomas de Tournon and Barthélemy Cavalier.

Among the charterhouse's greatest treasures must have been the *Coronation of the Virgin* by Enguerrand

Quarton. Originally from Laon in northern France, Quarton worked in the Flemish style which was dominant among Avignon painters in the fifteenth century. His *Pietà*, which was executed in Villeneuve but now hangs in the Louvre, is considered one of the finest fifteenth-century French paintings. The *Coronation*, which hangs in the Musée Municipal Pierre-de-Luxembourg, is unique in that the contract for its execution still survives. Drawn up on 24 April 1453, its twenty-six articles constitute a list of the painting's exact content. Although Quarton was contracted to depict the Carthusian vision of heaven and hell, it is stipulated that the method of execution should be 'to Master Enguerrand's liking' throughout. Quarton's Virgin, with her heavy-lidded eyes and

*E*nguerrand Quarton's *Coronation of the Virgin* (above) *is one of the masterpieces of the Avignon school. Working to a detailed contract, Quarton depicted the Trinity, with the Holy Ghost represented as a dove hovering over the Virgin's head. He was obliged to include St. Peter's and the Castel Sant'Angelo in Rome in the painting, but he also incorporated features from the local landscape* (opposite below) – *including Mont Ventoux. The figures to be represented in the crowd* (opposite above) *were also precisely listed in Quarton's contract.*

sensual mouth, is shown wearing a red cloak. Below her stands a crowd of onlookers depicted in such realistic detail that each one could have been painted from life. There are minute street scenes, with market stalls and tiny figures painted with a single brush stroke. Below this vision of wordly life lie hell and purgatory, depicted in all their glory, and sometimes comic detail.

The battlemented walls and towers of the Fort Saint-André form the backdrop to the charterhouse. Erected during the latter part of the fourteenth century, the fortress was conceived as an impressive symbol of French military strength. The portal that pierces its gargantuan walls is flanked by twin towers built in 1362. Inside the east tower you can visit the chambers that were used for many centuries to house prisoners. Their desperate graffiti are clearly visible on the walls.

Overleaf
*The light of early morning in Villeneuve-lès-Avignon reveals the powerful belfry of the collegiate church of Notre-Dame.*

# VAR & VAUCLUSE

*Bordered to the north-east by the Préalpes, Var has two great massifs: L'Esterel and Les Maures. The wild, forested landscape inland discouraged visitors for many centuries, but in the nineteenth century Hyères became the first Riviera resort. Standing among the ruins of the old château above the town, the contrast between the cluttered coastline to the south and the untouched foothills of Les Maures to the north is very vivid.*

*The variety of landscape encompassed by Vaucluse is extraordinary. Mountains, plateaux and gorges are all there, punctuated by gently sloping vineyards and olive groves. The area corresponds roughly to the Comtat Venaissin, the region claimed by the Pope in 1274, after the Albigensian Wars against the Cathars. Both Pernes-les-Fontaines and Carpentras served as temporary capitals of the Comtat, and the fascinating paraphernalia of papal government enriches the museums of towns throughout the region.*

*Although in the* département *of Drôme, just to the north of Vaucluse, Nyons is included in this section as the epitome of olive-growing Provence.*

*The pantiled roofs of houses surround the walls of the former collegiate church of Saint-Paul in Hyères.*

# *Carpentras*

VAUCLUSE

WITH ITS GRANDIOSE CIVIC BUILDINGS, narrow streets, lively markets and colourful history, Carpentras isn't a hard place to love. Of the four gates and thirty-two towers that once protected the town, only the Porte d'Orange survives. A shady boulevard on the site of the old fortifications siphons off the traffic, leaving the old town pleasantly quiet. The triumphal arch which stands against the north wall of the cathedral is a legacy of Roman occupation. Built in the first century A.D., it is decorated with bas-reliefs of two unfortunate barbarian prisoners dressed in animal skins.

In 1320 Carpentras became capital of the Comtat Venaissin. By that time, the region had been under papal rule for almost fifty years, and since 1309 the papal court had resided at Avignon. Clement V, formerly Archbishop of Bordeaux, was the first Pope to abandon Rome for Avignon. As a place to live, Avignon was neither peaceful nor healthy and Clement V preferred to spend much of his time in the castle at Monteux, not far from Carpentras.

The close connection between Carpentras and the papacy left its mark on the town. The fortifications, for example, were built on the orders of Pope Innocent VI, to protect the town from looting by mercenaries recruited during the Hundred Years War, but left redundant after the Treaty of Bretigny in 1360. Further

*T*his town delights both in detail and in the broader view: looking west from the top of the Porte d'Orange (left), and a sculpted fountain in the Place d'Inguimbert (above).

*There is plenty to catch the eye on the streets of Carpentras, like this painted façade on the Place du Général de Gaulle (opposite). There is more colour around the shops (left), richly stocked with local produce, and around the door of the concierge's house in the courtyard of the Bibliothèque Inguimbertine (far left).*

evidence is to be found in the Musée Comtadin, where glass cases overflow with seals, medals, edicts, coins and all the other paraphernalia of papal government. *Berlingots,* the humbug-shaped sweets sold all over Carpentras, are a more obscure relic from the past. Before his election to the papacy, Clement V was called Bertrand de Got, and *berlingot* is a corruption of his name. It is said that at a banquet held for Clement in 1313 the head *patissier* made miniature trees to stand at the centre of the table. Their branches were decked with candied and crystallized fruits which the guests were to pick and then eat with sweet custards. As a finishing touch, the *patissier* decorated the custards with threads of golden caramel. The *berlingots,* made on a whim to use up the remains of the caramelized sugar, have been produced in the town ever since.

The cathedral of Carpentras is the largest church in the diocese of Avignon. It was built on the orders of Benedict Xlll, one of the schismatic or anti-popes. Work began in 1404 on the site of three earlier

*Officially named the Passage Boyer, after an important citizen of the town, this nineteenth-century covered market (left) in the centre of Carpentras is universally known as the 'Rue Vitrée'.*

churches and took more than a century to complete. The south door, with its soaring pinnacles, is a magnificent example of the final phase of southern Gothic. Known as La Porte Juive (the Jewish Door), it was used by Jewish converts who came to the cathedral to be baptized. The cathedral is dedicated to St. Siffrein, Bishop of Carpentras between 557 and 570. Born into an aristocratic Italian family in 500, Siffrein is said to have been most unwilling to accept his appointment as bishop. He had been a monk on the island of Saint-Honorat, one of the Iles de Lérins off the coast of Cannes, since the age of ten, and he aspired to nothing more than a life of prayer and silence.

The church itself is a showcase for the work of Jacques Bernus, a brilliant sculptor born in Mazan in 1650. One of a family of artists, he refused to leave home in order to take up an apprenticeship in Italy. Instead, he became a pupil of Michel Peru of Avignon. The majority of the wooden carvings in the cathedral are by Bernus, commissioned by Laurent Buti, Bishop

*The eighteenth-century Hôtel-Dieu (opposite) is crowned by a magnificent triangular pediment topped by flaming torches; before it stands a statue of Bishop d'Inguimbert, the hospital's founder. Many of the treasures of the cathedral of Saint-Siffrein were destroyed during the Revolution. However, life-size angels in gilded wood (right) by local sculptor Jacques Bernus still stand on either side of the high altar. Beside the altar a painting on wood (below), dating from 1460, represents the crowning of the Virgin, St. Siffrein delivering a woman possessed, and St. Michael weighing souls.*

of Carpentras between 1691 and 1710. The gorgeously gilded wooden glory behind the high altar, rich with garlands, shells and festoons, imitates a work by Bernini. Never having been to Rome, Bernus had not seen the original; his inspiration was a print shown to him by Buti.

Two life-size angels kneeling on either side of the high altar are Bernus' masterpiece. They were saved during the Terror by the sculptor's quick-thinking nephew. In the face of a mob hell-bent on their destruction, he gave each angel a Phrygian cap and told the crowd that they were Republicans. Other treasures in the cathedral include paintings by Pierre Parrocel and Nicolas Mignard, artists of the Avignon school, and the Sacred Bit; the latter was said to be the bit made by the Emperor Constantine for his horse, using nails taken from the Cross.

The eighteenth century saw many fine new buildings erected in Carpentras. Malachie

d'Inguimbert, who was born in Carpentras and served as bishop between 1735 and 1757, was a generous benefactor. He founded a new hospital, the Hôtel-Dieu, just outside the city walls. He also left a magnificent collection of books and manuscripts to the town, which are housed in the Inguimbertine Library.

The Comtat Venaissin was a refuge for Jews persecuted elsewhere in France. The only trace left of the ghetto in the centre of Carpentras, however, is a magnificent synagogue. The original building dates from 1367, but the panelled sanctuary, with its subtle colours and *trompe-l'œil* paint-work, was completely restored in the eighteenth century. Despite papal tolerance of their presence, the Jews had very restricted lives. Their occupations were severely controlled and they were forced to live in the cramped ghettos of only four towns, Carpentras, Cavaillon, Avignon and L'Isle-sur-la-Sorgue.

*The cathedral's magnificent Porte Juive (left) was used by converted Jews to enter the christening chapel where new converts could be baptised. Standing on the site of the old ghetto, the Synagogue (above) was built between 1741 and 1743 by Antoine d'Allemand. Its inconspicuous façade conceals a well-appointed interior. Looking east from the Porte d'Orange, the spire of Notre-Dame-de-l'Observance is seen against the unmistakable backdrop of Mont Ventoux (opposite).*

# Hyères

VAR

LONG AFTER WINTER WEATHER has stopped play inland, Hyères continues to live out its perpetual summer. The tables still stand outside bars on the squares; the houses in the steep streets remain swathed in colourful bougainvillaea. Hyères may not have its own sea-front, but it is drenched in the Riviera light that brings needle-sharp clarity to the vision, as if one had been granted perfect eyesight overnight. It was this light and its accompanying warmth which brought tourists to Hyères in the eighteenth and nineteenth centuries, turning it into the very first resort on the Côte d'Azur. The guest list is long and illustrious, including Napoleon, the Empress Josephine, Pauline Borghese and Queen Victoria, who was photographed sitting in a dog-cart in the grounds of the Grand Hotel. The pony in the shafts is a Shetland that she had brought with her from England.

The town and the unspoilt countryside around it also attracted writers – Tolstoy, Maupassant and Victor Hugo among them. The American novelist Edith Wharton became a permanent resident in 1927,

*Bathed in morning light, Hyères* (left) *sits prettily on its hill against the wooded backdrop of the Massif des Maures. In the heart of the old town delightfully contrived details meet the visitor at every turn* (above).

85

*The houses of the Rue Barbacane (opposite) are painted in the soft pastels typical of the Riviera. Saint-Louis (right) was once the church of a Franciscan convent; its elegant façade, punctuated by three round arches and a rose-window, hovers in style between Romanesque and Provençal Gothic.*

Overleaf
*The Villa Mauresque (p.88), on the Rue Jean Natte, and the Villa Tunisienne (p.89), on the Avenue Andrée-David de Beauregard, were among the results of the flurry of new building which accompanied the development of Hyères as a luxurious winter resort. These confections of neo-Moorish arches, crenellations and patterned tiles were designed at the end of the nineteenth century by local architect P. Chapoulart.*

when she moved into the converted convent of Sainte-Claire-le-Château, high above the town. Finally, like all the towns of the Riviera, Hyères had its share of tuberculosis patients, although it is hard to imagine how they coped with the precipitous streets of the old town. Robert Louis Stevenson was one such visitor. He came twice during the 1880s on the advice of his doctor, and stayed in a house lent to him by Edith Wharton. Years later he said to his old friend Sidney Colvin, 'I have only ever been happy once and that was in Hyères'. Colvin was so struck by Stevenson's

attachment to the place that he recorded the remark in his *Memories and Notes of Persons and Places, 1852–1912.*

Hyères was at its most powerful during the Middle Ages, when it was the headquarters of the Knights Templar, one of the great crusading orders whose members took monastic vows but lived as soldiers. Their presence brought status to the little town, and also wealth, for they ran a lucrative sideline as international financiers. The Tour Saint-Blaise, a massive structure that dominates the pretty Place Massillon in the heart of the town, is all that remains

of their commandery. From the top of the tower there is a breathtaking view of the sea, only 5 kilometres away, and the tightly packed streets of the old town that climb the hillside. The ruins of Hyères' castle can just be seen at the top of the hill. It was this castle, built by the lords of Fos at the beginning of the Middle Ages, that drew Hyères' first inhabitants away from the coast to build their houses in the protective shadow of the castle wall. The ruins visible today date from the thirteenth century, when the castle was rebuilt by the Counts of Provence.

At the foot of the Templars' tower is the Place Massillon, a busy market square lined with houses and restaurants painted in bright, Riviera colours. The square and the city gate nearby are named after Jean-Baptiste Massillon, Bishop of Clermont, who was born in the town in 1662. Famed for his preaching, Massillon is said to have provoked Louis XIV to say, 'Each time I hear him, I become discontented with myself.'

The collegiate church of Saint-Paul is built on a steep incline at the heart of the old town. The original building was twelfth-century and the square bell-tower, which can really only be appreciated from behind the building, is pure Romanesque. The church is reached up a steep flight of sixteenth-century steps. A first glance at the interior suggests that it has been deconsecrated and turned into an art gallery. Closer inspection reveals that the paintings covering the walls from top to bottom are all ex-voto offerings, a collection that has been accumulating since the seventeenth century. They depict every possible near-death experience, including the lucky survival of an eighteenth-month-old baby who fell head first into a water-barrel. The paintings span five centuries, and yet they are all similarly naive in style. Ex-votos were rarely produced by professional painters. They were a sideline for craftsmen - such as picture-framers or house-painters - who stuck to a simple, centuries-old formula.

*Overlooking one of the small ports that serve the Îles d'Hyères, the Tour Fondue (above) was built in the seventeenth century to control the narrows of La Petite Passe. In the town itself the Fontaine Godillot (left) stands on the avenue of the same name; Alexis Godillot, whose wealth derived from supplying arms to the Second Empire, once owned a quarter of Hyères, which he re-christened Hyères-les-Palmiers. In the Place Massillon (opposite) café tables await their first customers in the morning sunlight.*

# L'Isle-sur-la-Sorgue

VAUCLUSE

L'ISLE-SUR-LA-SORGUE SITS ON THE PLAIN at the western end of the Vaucluse plateau. Its name is a simple statement of fact, for the town is entirely encircled by the clear and miraculously cold waters of the river Sorgue. Even on the hottest summer's day, a breath of cool air rises from the water. Fig trees self-seed in the damp walls of the water channels all over the town, lending their shade to narrow streets, where small boys playing football are more of a hazard than traffic.

The Sorgue is a river much given to partings and reunions. It surges from a chasm of impossible depths at Fontaine-de-Vaucluse. Between there and L'Isle-sur-la-Sorgue, a distance of less than 10 kilometres, it divides five times. René Char, the Surrealist poet who was born and brought up in the town, described it as the 'river too soon parted…without a companion'. Just outside the town, one can stand at the first watershed and observe the river dividing itself neatly in half, as at a cross-roads. It makes one wonder about the lives of the fish in these parts!

It is hardly surprising that the inhabitants of the earliest settlement at L'Isle should have been fishermen. Flat-bottomed boats, called *nego-chin* in dialect, were traditionally used in these waters. They are still made locally and can be commissioned – at a price. The town controlled exclusive rights to the fishing as far as the Rhône, and by the Middle Ages the townspeople had begun to put the river to sophisticated use. They harnessed the rushing water to power the paddle-wheels of mills, and as a result,

*The river Sorgue flows beneath the Pont Gambetta at the Quai Jean-Jaurès; the quais which surround the town follow the line of the town walls, round which the river flowed.*

*P*opular with artists and lovers alike, the town's public gardens (opposite) occupy the south bank of the Sorgue. The centre of the old town is dominated by the sixteenth-century bell-tower (below) of Notre-Dame-des-Anges in the Place de la Liberté. The interior of the church (right) is a sumptuous affair of seventeenth-century Baroque ornament; statues of the divine, moral and cardinal virtues line the nave.

L'Isle-sur-la-Sorgue gradually became a manufacturing centre. By the nineteenth century there were seventy mills in the town. Paper-making was most important, but there was also a silk and textile industry, flour-milling, dying, tanning, and olive oil production. Giant mill-wheels crop up unexpectedly all over the town, their inexorably turning paddles swathed in viridian weed.

Following a familiar pattern, the rich mill-owners built themselves magnificent town houses. The Hôtel-Dieu on the Rue Jean-Théophile was built in 1757. Its grand entrance-hall and the massive wall-fountain in the quiet garden behind it speak eloquently of the fine living to be made from industry in the eighteenth century.

The industrialists were not the only people to generate wealth for L'Isle-sur-la-Sorgue. The town's prosperity was also due to the commercial success of the Jewish community. When the Comtat Venaissin came under papal control in 1274 it became a haven for Jews and other groups escaping persecution. Although they were not actively persecuted in the region, however, the Jews still lived very restricted lives. By the eighteenth century L'Isle-sur-la-Sorgue was one of only four towns in which they were permitted to live. By the end of the eighteenth century there were about 300 Jews living in L'Isle. The ghetto was a single street which was completely sealed by a locked gate each night. It was demolished, along with the synagogue, in the nineteenth century, and all that remains is the name, Place de la Juiverie.

Most of the main streets in L'Isle-sur-la-Sorgue lead to the Place de la Liberté, and the huge, slightly crumbling church of Notre-Dame-des-Anges. Although Gothic in origin, the building was completely remodelled in the seventeenth century by François Royer de la Valfrenière, who also designed the Palais de Justice (Continued on p.100)

Overleaf
*Some private residences near the Avenue des Quatre Otages are reached by foot-bridges.*

*N*ow an antiques store, this building (left) once housed one of L'Isle-sur-la-Sorgue's innumerable mills. There is no shortage of pleasant places to have a drink or watch the town go by: tables set out in the shade on the Quai Jean-Jaurès (below), and outside the Café de France (opposite) in the Place de la Liberté.

in Carpentras and the Museé Lapidaire in Avignon. It was consecrated in its present form in 1672 by the Bishop of Cavaillon. The magnificently opulent Baroque interior includes a number of statues carved in poplar by Jean Peru and arranged along the north and south sides of the nave. In the side chapels there are paintings by Nicolas Mignard and Pierre Parrocel.

*The vast waterwheel (right) on the Cours Victor Hugo is a vivid memorial to the industries that brought wealth to L'Isle-sur-la-Sorgue. The growth of water-powered industries continued until the end of the nineteenth century, roughly the date of this shop sign (below) on the Avenue des Quatre Otages.*

# Nyons

## DRÔME

ANCIENT OLIVE TREES HERALD the approach to Nyons from the south. To the west, beyond the trees and the ice-blue water of the Eygues, Nyons can be seen against its hill, encircled and enclosed on all sides by Les Baronnies, the hills that define the eastern end of the Tricastin plain. Above the town, olives grow on terraces cut from the hillside. Elsewhere, the sharp, forested spines of Les Baronnies intersect to form innumerable sheltered valleys where yet more olives grow.

Nyons is built at the point where the river Eygues emerges from a gorge and rushes on to the plain. Two bridges cross the water, the modern Pont de l'Europe and, a short distance upstream, the elegant Pont Roman. Built between 1341 and 1409, the latter leads into the Quartier des Forts, an intricate web of narrow streets that spreads across the hillside. At times, the streets give way to steep flights of steps or covered galleries known as *soustets*. The finest of these is the Rue des Grands-Forts, a dark tunnel lit occasionally by narrow windows. In some places the streets pierce the curtain walls of the feudal castle, the *fort* that gives the

*The distinctive iron bell-cage of Saint-Vincent (above) is one of the outstanding features of old Nyons, spread out beneath the wooded backdrop of Les Baronnies (left).*

*The Pont Roman across the river Eygues (opposite) was built by the medieval Frères Hospitaliers Pontifs, a body of men pledged to bridge-building, caring for ferries, and helping travellers across dangerous rivers and fords. In summer, the quiet waters of the Eygues (below) are popular with fishermen. On the river bank west of the bridge is the Jardin des Arômes, where essential oils are distilled from the aromatic plants that grow there (left). Groves of venerable olive trees (far left) surround the town.*

area its name, and in others they create a tiny channel between the towering walls of fourteenth-century houses. The castle was built in the eighth century to protect the monastery of Saint-Vincent. The eleventh century saw its transformation into a more elegant château, lived in by the barons of Montauban.

The Tour Randonne stands half-way up the hill. Built in 1280 by Dame Randonne-de-Montauban, it was originally designed as a military prison. Like the rest of Nyons' fortifications, it was largely demolished in 1633. Today, it is almost entirely concealed by the tiny chapel of Notre-Dame-de-Bon-Secours, built above it in the nineteenth century and then capped with the elaborate neo-Gothic belfry that dominates views of the town. Above the tower, the narrow, twisting streets are bathed in sunlight. Mimosa, palm and citrus trees grow in minute gardens while succulents thrive among the hot rocks. These tender Riviera plants bring an unexpected, seaside

*Nyons is a place of contrasts, of sun-drenched streets (opposite) and dark vaulted passages, like the Rue des Grands-Forts (left). A remaining tower of the town wall, dismantled with Nyons' other fortifications in 1633, still rises above the Rue Pierre Toesca (below). At the foot of the old town is the pleasant Place des Arcades – a good place to buy a loaf of bread (below left).*

atmosphere to Nyons. They flourish in a microclimate created by the sheltering bowl of Les Baronnies. The town and the land around are spared the ravages of the Mistral; as a result, the winter temperature rarely falls below 5°C. The only persistent wind is a morning breeze called the Pontias, which is the subject of a local legend. The hero of the story is St. Caesarius, Bishop of Arles at the beginning of the sixth century. A popular preacher, he was founder of the first known convent of women in Gaul. Among the rules of the new house, where his sister was abbess, it was stipulated that each nun should learn to read and write. These facts are all well-documented - unlike the rest of this story. It is said that he captured a puff of sea air in his glove and released it over Nyons. The wind was trapped by the surrounding hills and for evermore a refreshing breeze blew there each morning.

The olive trees that cover the countryside around Nyons thrive in the mild climate. In other areas of Provence the extreme frosts of 1956, 1985 and 1990 exterminated eighty per cent of the olives. Although it did not escape unscathed, Nyons fared better than most areas north of the coast, and as a result it has some of the oldest olive groves in Provence.

Nyons' olives are largely of the *tanche* variety, a heart-shaped fruit of medium size. Picked in December when slightly overripe, the *tanche* yields an oil the colour of burnished bronze. The oil made in Nyons has its own *appellation*, and is reckoned among some of the most precious in Provence.

*Standing in the shelter of the hills, Nyons catches the evening sun* (left); *every part of the town is dominated by the neo-Gothic Tour Randonne* (above).

# Pernes-les-Fontaines

VAUCLUSE

*The former keep of the castle of the Counts of Toulouse, now known as the Tour de l'Horloge, provides sweeping views across the town (opposite). Another tower, the Tour Ferrande, houses graphic thirteenth-century frescoes on its third floor (above).*

Pernes-les-Fontaines' moments of power were short-lived. From 1274 to 1320 it was the capital of the Comtat Venaissin, the region surrounding Avignon that was under papal control. Although Carpentras soon took over as regional capital, the little town has never lost its air of importance. Today, most commercial activity takes place on plane-lined avenues outside the city walls. Inside, the medieval façades of the houses remain virtually untouched by the modern world.

The fountains that lend their name to the place post-date Pernes' era of glory by more than 400 years.

It was only in 1936 that Perne had 'les-Fontaines' added to its title. There are thirty-six fountains in all, scattered among the narrow streets and squares of the old town. They were built to celebrate the abundant supply of water provided by the irrigation of the Comtat plain in the eighteenth century. Most of them are the small wall-fountains that are to be found in so many Provençal towns or villages. Of the free-standing ones, the fountain of the cormorant (Fontaine du Cormoran) just inside the Porte Notre-Dame is probably the finest. The bird is frozen in the instant before it swallows the fish in its beak.

The beautiful, pale sandstone Porte Notre-Dame is one of three gates that lead through the town walls. It is linked to a fine cobbled bridge that spans the river Nesque, a tributary of the Sorgue. Willows and plane trees cast their shade over the wide, gravelled walk that runs along the river. When the air cools in the late afternoon, this is the spot where the boule players gather. The pretty, pantiled chapel of Notre-Dame-des-Graces is built on one of the piles of the bridge, just a few yards from the fine church of Notre-Dame-de-Nazareth. During the building and rebuilding of the town walls in the fourteenth and sixteenth centuries, the twelfth-century church was left outside the town boundary.

*The Tour de l'Horloge also offers a view towards the Dentelles de Montmirail (above), a range of foothills so-called because its fine spikes and ridges bear a resemblance to the edges of a piece of lace ('dentelle').*

*A*s its name implies, Pernes is a town of fountains, thirty-six in all, most of them created in the eighteenth century as part of the irrigation scheme for the plain of Comtat. Some are simple wall spouts (this page), while others are elaborate sculpted works, like the Fontaine du Gigot, which plays in the tiny square beneath the crenellated Tour Ferrande (opposite below).

*The sun-dappled streets of the town* (preceding pages) *provide a tranquil counter-note to its grander monuments: the great Fontaine du Cormoran* (above) *and eleventh-century Notre-Dame-de-Nazareth* (right).

Pernes' spacious, seventeenth-century covered market stands against the inside of the town wall, right next to the Porte Notre-Dame. A cane, once the official unit of measure, is still fastened to the wall. The thirteenth-century Tour Ferrande is thought to have belonged to the Knights Hospitallers, the crusading order that also had the special duty of caring for the sick and wounded on the battlefield. Inside the tower, the top storey is decorated with a series of late thirteenth-century frescoes which give a vivid, pictorial account of the conquest of Sicily by Charles of Anjou. Another thirteenth-century building is a clock-tower which soars above the roofs of the town. This is all that remains of a castle which once belonged to the Counts of Toulouse; the clock itself was installed in 1496, but the ornate wrought-iron belfry only dates from 1764.

# ALPES-MARITIMES & ALPES-DE-HAUTE-PROVENCE

*A drive of less than an hour will take you from the unspoilt Riviera resort of Menton to the little alpine town of Sospel. The* département *of Alpes-Maritimes is one of the most varied in Provence. Stretching from the remote, haunting valleys of the north to the Italian border, it also encompasses the rich tourist belt of the Côte d'Azur, with its mild climate and luxuriant vegetation. Alpes-Maritimes was only created in 1860 on the annexation of the* comté *of Nice to France. But a distinctive, Italianate twist still distinguishes the architecture, food and dialects of the towns close to the eastern border.*

*Alpes-de-Haute-Provence is the name given to one of the wildest areas of the whole Midi. This mountainous region in the north-east of Provence was the inspiration for the author Jean Giono (1895–1970), who lived for most of his life in Manosque and wrote of the austere plateaux and desolate, deserted villages there. Bordered to the west by the arid slopes of the Montagne de Lure, it is dominated by the Plateau de Valensole, Giono's 'magnificent friend'. The lavender that has been cultivated in Provence since the nineteenth century transforms the plateau into a hazy, purple sea in the July of each year. Grasse, Sisteron and Digne are all sited in different sections of the dramatic landscape known as the Préalpes. Beyond Sisteron, however, the landscape takes on a truly alpine character which has more in common with Savoy than Provence.*

*The Rue Mirabeau in Grasse; in the foreground is the town's museum devoted to the art and history of Provence.*

# Grasse

ALPES-MARITIMES

BUILT ON A HILLSIDE only twelve miles from the Mediterranean coast, Grasse is an old Provençal town of towering buildings and narrow streets linked by steep flights of steps. Despite a successful tourist industry, it retains the busy atmosphere of a real town with an absorbing life of its own. Each morning a flower and vegetable market is set up around an elegant fountain in the arcaded Place aux Aires, once the centre of the town's lucrative tanning industry. Even at the height of summer, the tourists attracted to this beautiful scene are outnumbered by local people who gather each day to shop and gossip.

Grasse is the self-styled 'Capital of the Perfume Industry', a name amply justified by the thirty businesses that operate in the area. Already renowned for their glove-making, the tanners of Grasse were well-placed to respond to the Italian fashion for scented leather that took Europe by storm in the sixteenth century. Many of the aromatic plants that they needed were to be found growing wild on the rocky slopes above the town. Until quite recently, the plain below Grasse was given over to the cultivation of roses and jasmine. All the flowers were hand-picked, though eventually this proved prohibitively expensive. Jasmine, a nocturnal flowerer, was particularly problematic, as it could only be gathered between four in the morning and noon. Now, much of the land has been sold for development and the perfume factories now import their ingredients from India, Madagascar and Egypt.

The cathedral of Notre-Dame-du-Puy is probably Grasse's most important building. The original edifice was completely refurbished when the town became the centre of a bishopric in 1244 and later substantially

*The town, caught here in the light of sunrise, lies under the dominating presence of its cathedral of Notre-Dame-du-Puy.*

Preceding pages
*A twelfth-century watchtower, the Tour de Guet, rises just in front of the cathedral (p.122). The Place de la Poissonnerie (p.123) was originally the site of a fish market, as its name indicates.*

*Among the treasures of the cathedral are a carved figure of St. Jerome (below right) and a triptych of 1523–24 (left), attributed to Louis Bréa; it shows St. Honoratus, flanked by St. Clement and St. Lambert. Outside, the double perron (below left) was added during the eighteenth century; within, the marks of a fire of 1795 can still be discerned on the pillars of the narrow nave (opposite).*

modified in the seventeenth century. The façade is a magnificent specimen of the sober, Lombard style that crept over the border from Italy into Provence. It is almost bereft of decoration, although a frieze of blind arches, a Lombard arcade, decorates the roof-line. A double staircase, or *perron*, was added in the eighteenth century. Inside, the vast, shadowy ceiling of the nave is supported by vaults with the square-section ribs typical of the period.

Among the cathedral's treasures is a beautiful altar-piece by Louis Bréa, a Niçois painter whose work owed more to the influence of Italy than France. Paintings by Rubens, executed in 1601, hang in the cathedral. Originally commissioned (Continued on p.130)

The Route Napoléon, the road taken by the Emperor in March 1815 after his escape from Elba, goes north from the town. Napoleon, commemorated by this roadside bust (right), decided to avoid the centre of Grasse after a hostile reception in Cannes, and skirted the town on what is now the Boulevard du Jeu de Ballon (below). These roses on the Montée du Casino (opposite) aptly reflect the traditional business of Grasse, for the rose has been at the heart of its perfume industry for over two hundred years. Each May, the Festival of the Rose celebrates the flower in a series of concerts and exhibitions. A statue (below right) to the town's most famous son, Jean-Honoré Fragonard, stands in the Square du Clavecin; his name has been adopted by one of the most important perfumeries of Grasse.

Overleaf

Perfume is not the only business of Grasse: seemingly almost anything can be bought from this ironmonger's in the Rue de la Poissonnerie (p.128). The Rue Tracastel (p.129) took its name from the Latin, retro castellum, referring to its location outside the defences of the medieval town.

*Grasse is a town which seems to curl around its cathedral (opposite), seen here beyond improbably lofty palm trees. Its many levels demand stairways, like this one leading to the Place du 24 Août (left), and reveal delightful façades, like this one of a house on the Boulevard Fragonard (above).*

for Santa Croce di Gerusalemme in Rome, they are *St. Helena and the Exaltation of the Holy Cross*, *The Raising of the Cross* and *Christ Crowned with Thorns*. The paintings are on wood and have suffered considerable damage from the damp atmosphere of the cathedral.

In the chapel of the Holy Sacrament hangs Jean-Honoré Fragonard's painting of *Christ Washing the Feet of the Apostles*. Born in Grasse in 1732, Fragonard lost most of his aristocratic patrons and subjects during the Revolution; by the time of his death in 1806, he had been all but forgotten. Significantly for this town, Fragonard's father had been a manufacturer of perfumed gloves in the early eighteenth century; the

name was later adopted by one of the principal perfume companies of Grasse. Among Carthaginian, Roman and Greek exhibits in the magnificent museum of the company are samples of the ingredients that go into the manufacture of perfume today: no place for the romantic or the faint-hearted.

Although it was not on the coast, the mild winter climate of Grasse made it as alluring to northern visitors as the seaside towns of the Riviera. When Queen Victoria visited it in 1891 she travelled through France on the Royal Train. Supplies for the journey included mutton stew which was kept at blood heat in a nest of red-flannel cushions.

# Menton

## ALPES-MARITIMES

CAUGHT BETWEEN the rocky foot-hills of the Alpes-Maritimes and the great expanse of the Mediterranean, Menton is the most Italianate town of the Côte d'Azur. In the shops and cafés conversation slips seamlessly between French and Italian, sometimes changing in mid-sentence, as though the speakers made no real distinction between the two languages.

The steep steps and winding alleyways of the old town cover a rocky hillside rising from the sea. Further along the coast, the building boom of the nineteen-sixties and seventies has left its distinctive imprint, but in Menton itself the ochre-coloured houses and tunnel-like, cobbled streets remain untouched. Here, at the heart of the town, stands Saint-Michel, the finest of Menton's churches, in a square decorated with an elaborate pebble mosaic of the Grimaldi coat of arms. The Grimaldi family, the Princes of Monaco, bought Menton in 1346 and continued their rule until 1848. It was said that the final years of Grimaldi rule were an uncomfortable period of constant police surveillance, high taxes and monopolies benefiting nobody but the Prince.

Saint-Michel is one of the finest Baroque churches of the whole region. The first stone was laid in 1611 by the Bishop of Ventimiglia at a ceremony attended by Prince Honoré II of Monaco, but progress was slow

*The eighteenth-century Italianate campanile of Saint-Michel, towering above the huddled houses of the town, is the dominant landmark of Menton (right). Menton's marriages are sealed in a room decorated by Jean Cocteau (above).*

and the building was not consecrated until 1675. The two-tier façade is decorated with statues. St. Michael, patron saint of Menton, slays Lucifer above the door. To either side of him stand St. Roche, whose name is invoked as protection against the plague, and St. Maurice. The fifteenth-century tower to the east of the façade was part of an earlier building. It was crowned with a magnificent octagonal campanile with a colourful, glazed-tile roof in the seventeenth century. On the other side of the façade is the Genoese campanile that was built between 1701 and 1703. Its graceful cupola dominates views of the old town from all directions.

The sumptuous interior of Saint-Michel was inspired by that of Santissima Annunziata in Genoa. It is infused with a rich light, due in part to the red Genoese damask hangings that cover the walls. They were hung there in 1757 at the instigation of Prince Honoré III, when Saint-Michel was the setting for his marriage to a Genoese princess. The altar-piece above the eighteenth-century choir stalls is by Antoine Manchello, a painter from Monaco. It depicts St. Michael and is signed and dated 1565. The side chapels, which contain paintings by local artists, are dedicated to the memory of powerful families, such as the Grimaldi, the Saint-Ambroise and the Monléon.

*Viewed from any angle, the streets of Menton (these pages) feel almost more Italian than French; campaniles, colonnades and ornamental palms make the town one of the jewels of the Mediterranean coastline.*

Preceding pages
*Menton is a town of many levels: the Rampes du Chanoine Gouget (p.134), by Saint-Michel; the steps leading to the Chapelle de la Conception (p.135), church of the Pénitents Blancs, its façade completed by statues of the three theological virtues.*

*Look anywhere in Menton, and some fascinating detail will delight the eye: a still-life with table and plant by the church of Saint-Michel (opposite); colonnade and frieze in the gardens of the Fontana Rosa (right); and tempting produce laid out on the stalls of the famous covered market (below).*

Among the church's treasures is a Turkish spear, brought back from the Battle of Lepanto by Mentonese soldiers. Outside, a short flight of steps leads to the Place de la Conception. Here, the Chapelle des Pénitents Blancs is also Baroque, and dates from 1685.

The quiet streets of the old town lead up to the cemetery, a site that reflects one of the most important periods in Menton's history. Foreign graves predominate, and the gravestones, most of them nineteenth- or early twentieth-century, bear witness to hundreds of lives cut short after only twenty or thirty years. These are the graves of the tuberculosis patients who flocked to Menton each winter in search of a climate that would alleviate their condition. Among them were artists and writers such as Aubrey Beardsley, Robert Louis Stevenson and Katherine Mansfield.

The town's popularity as a winter resort for invalids was due initially to a book published by Dr.

James Bennet. Suffering from tuberculosis himself, Bennet had gone to Menton in 1859 'to die in a quiet corner'. To his surprise, he found that his condition improved. In 1861 he published *Mentone and the Riviera as a Winter Climate*, the book that was to advertise the benefits of escaping the harsh, northern winters for the mild climate of the French Riviera. In the fourteen years that elapsed before his book was reprinted Menton changed from a quiet little town with three hotels, to 'a well-known and frequented winter resort, with 30 hotels, four times that number of villas and a mixed foreign population of above 1,600'. For an economy that had depended almost entirely on the cultivation of lemons, the transformation was remarkable.

Although an American book entitled *Montecarlo and How To Do It*, published in 1891, described the residents of Menton as 'being of a bronchial nature, suggestive of Bournemouth, apt to cough and spit in a manner that does not act as a gin-and-bitters to your next meal', not all of the foreign visitors were invalids. Each year, there was a mass winter migration of aristocracy from all over Europe. Russian grand dukes and duchesses were among the crowds that flocked to Menton and the other coastal towns of the Riviera, entrusting the local police force with the arduous task of protecting them from assassination. Queen Victoria was another regular visitor. The magnificent Belle Époque palaces and hotels that line the coast and the Garavan are the legacy of this period.

*B*oth defensive and decorative (above *and* right), *Menton is a former frontier town which has blossomed into today's sophisticated resort.*

# Saint-Martin-Vésubie

ALPES-MARITIMES

A TINY JEWEL OF A TOWN, Saint-Martin-Vésubie clusters around a main street, the cobbled Rue du Docteur-Cagnoli, lined by handsome Gothic houses with overhanging roofs, fine porches and balconies. A narrow gutter runs down the centre of the street; originally designed as an open sewer in the fifteenth century, it now channels ice-cold water from the top of the town to the bottom. The sound of running water that fills the street is echoed and amplified by the wall-fountains to be found all over the town.

Saint-Martin stands at the head of the Vésubie, a river formed by the two torrents of the Boréon and the Madone de Fenestre. At 975 metres (3200 feet) the living can be harsh and the town's inhabitants have come to rely heavily on the income brought by summer walkers and climbers. These visitors are drawn in part by the town's position on the southern edge of

the magnificent Parc National du Mercantour, a vast tract of mountain landscape where marmots, ibex, moufflons, eagles, ptarmigans and even wolves thrive in a protected environment. Two thousand species of flowering plant have been recorded in the Mercantour, forty of them unique to the area. The park also encompasses the Vallée des Merveilles, one of the most important prehistoric sites in Europe. Lying between two glacial lakes on the western flank of Mont Bégo, it is covered by snow from autumn until spring and this has protected thousands of images that were incised into the rocks during the Bronze Age. Some of them are obscure symbols, but others are readily recognizable animals, tools and human figures.

The chapels of the Black and White Penitents are among the most important buildings in Saint-Martin. The Penitents, who wore black, white or grey hooded

*The town of Saint-Martin lies in the deep valley of the Vésubie* (opposite), *overlooked by mist-enveloped Venanson* (above).

*The iconoclasm of the Revolution hardly seems to have touched the churches of Saint-Martin: the chapel of the Black Penitents, the Chapelle de la Miséricorde, retains its elaborate Baroque interior (this page). The main church, Notre-Dame-de-l'Assomption, also retains a distinctive seventeenth-century air, thanks to this splendid altarpiece (opposite).*

gowns, were established all over the Midi from the thirteenth century onwards. They were lay, charitable organizations, often patronized by nobility and even royalty. In Saint-Martin there are records of both Black and White Penitents from the seventeenth century onwards, although it is thought that their presence dates back to the sixteenth century.

The Chapelle des Pénitents Blancs stands on the Rue du Docteur-Cagnoli. The building dates from the end of the seventeenth century, but the Neoclassical façade was added in 1850. The White Penitents of Saint-Martin made a good living by trading with the Piedmontese over the Italian border. They also owned a lot of land which they rented out, yielding revenue which allowed them to contribute to the cultural life of the town, to distribute alms and, most significantly, to found and support a hospital. The brotherhood continued to operate in Saint-Martin until the beginning of the twentieth century. The interior of their chapel is gloriously painted in midnight blue, gold and burnt orange. A recumbent figure of Christ creates a focal point beneath the altar. The richly

Notre-Dame-de-l'Assomption, the parish church, stands with its back to the town, its Baroque façade turned to the rushing torrent of the Madone de Finestre and the peaks of the Palu and the Piagu. The church has had a turbulent history. Fires started by careless travellers using the building as a shelter caused considerable damage in 1665, 1838, 1846 and 1883. The twelfth-century polychrome Madonna that stands to the right of the choir miraculously survived each time in spite of being carved in wood. Every year a procession transports the figure to the chapel of the Madone de Fenestre in the barren, rocky landscape to the north-east of the town. In September, before the first snowfall, the Madonna is returned to Saint-Martin.

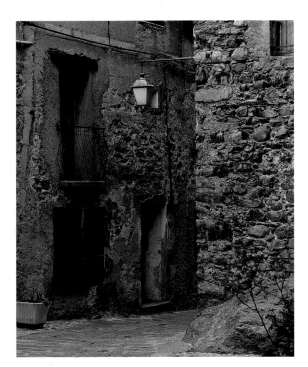

carved and painted figure is worked in a style characteristic of the region. Eighteenth-century paintings depicting the Stations of the Cross hang on the walls.

The Chapelle des Pénitents Noirs originally served as the parish church of Saint-Martin. It stands outside the fifteenth-century walls of the town on the site of an earlier building. The Black Penitents worked with bereaved families in the town, their income deriving from the contributions of noble members and from the grain that they collected in lieu of rent on their land. Over the altar of the chapel hangs a painting of the beheading of John the Baptist by an unknown artist. A chain on the saint's ankle is a reference to the Penitents' privilege of pardoning one condemned man each year; after such an intercession, the captive's sentence would be transmuted to life-imprisonment.

*The steeply pitched roofs of the houses on the Rue du Docteur-Cagnoli (above) lend Saint-Martin a distinctly alpine atmosphere. And even in early summer, this tiny town of intimate corners (this page) and vertiginously rising apartments (opposite) remains surrounded by snow fields.*

# Sospel

ALPES-MARITIMES

Standing in the Place Saint-Michel, looking up at the beautiful, ochre-painted Baroque façade of the church, it would be easy to imagine yourself in Italy. The whole character, cooking and dialect of the place has been defined by nearly 600 years of Italian rule under the Counts of Savoy. By 1860, when Italy was unified and Nice was at last annexed to France, Sospel's position remained unchanged. Despite local opinion, Victor Emmanuel II, Italy's new king, refused to sacrifice the hunting that he so enjoyed in the wild, wooded country around the town. It was not until 1947 that the valley was finally handed over to France.

Built between 1641 and 1762, Saint-Michel is the largest church in the Alpes-Maritimes. The glorious, crumbling excesses of the Baroque interior reflect its original status as a cathedral. All that remains of the earlier basilica is a Romanesque bell-tower which stands next to a beautiful, medieval arcade. The cathedral's greatest treasure is an *Assumption* painted by François Bréa in 1520. Bréa was one of a flourishing Niçois family of painters. His resplendent Virgin is set against a richly detailed landscape which has more in common with the styles of northern and central Italy than France.

Outside, the cathedral is flanked by the chapels of the Red and Grey Penitents on one side, and the Palais Ricci with its *trompe-l'œil* decoration on the other. The overall effect is that of a sparse but perfect opera set. Underfoot, the square is paved with a star-shaped pattern of grey and white stones. These were originally dredged from the gentle river Bévéra that divides the town in two. The south bank, with its fine cathedral, dark streets and Baroque palaces, was developed when the *comté* of Nice was annexed to the newly created Kingdom of Sardinia. These were the town's glory days, a time of great wealth and expansion.

*An eleventh-century bridge, complete with toll tower, joins the two halves of the town, which stretch out along either bank of the river Bévéra.*

149

The development of the Bévéra's south bank threw the existing, medieval settlement of Saint-Nicolas, on the opposite side of the river, into eclipse. It had reached the height of its power in the thirteenth century, when the Counts of Provence made it the headquarters for their army. The ruined remains of their castle can still be seen on the Rue de l'Abbaye, above the Place Saint-Michel.

The salt route from Nice to Turin ran through Saint-Nicolas. For centuries, dusty caravans of mules trudged through the town, hauling their precious cargo from the salt-marshes of the Provençal coast to Turin and returning weeks later laden with Piedmontese rice; the salt road was effectively the town's main street, lined by an arcade of shops. Today, the street is the Rue de la République; its medieval arcade is still there, although all the shops closed in the eighteenth century. Running off it to the north is the Rue des Tisserands, or 'weavers' alley'. Like the salt warehouses in the Place de la Cabraïa, it is a reminder of Saint-Nicolas' medieval wealth, earned in part by the silk spun from the cocoons of silkworms raised on mulberry trees in the fertile valley of the Bévéra.

*The Romanesque bell-tower of Saint-Michel stands strangely with the Baroque façade of the church (opposite). Baroque, too, is its interior (above right), remarkable for its denticular corniche and an altarpiece of the Virgin Mary by François Bréa (above). Slightly less grand is the Chapelle des Pénitents Blancs de la Sainte-Croix (right).*

*General views of Sospel can disguise the fact that this is also a place of charming detail: trompe-l'œil façades along the Bévéra* (left); *Henri Raibaut, the ironmonger of the Place Saint-Michel* (below left); *and the baker's on the Place Saint-Nicolas* (below right).

*D*espite the name on this bar and newsagent's on the Avenue Jean Médecin (right), *much of Sospel's charm is derived from a sense that it has been sheltered from the modern world. In the Place Saint-Michel an upholsterer goes about his traditional trade outside his shop* (above). *This eighteenth-century fountain* (above right), *in the arcade that runs beneath the Hôtel de Ville on the Place Saint-Nicolas, used to be the meeting-place for the local officials of Sospel.*

Saint-Nicolas is linked to the main town of Sospel
by a fine, twin-arched stone bridge built in the
sixteenth century. A tower and a toll house stand in
the middle, giving the structure a unique profile.
Badly damaged by retreating German troops in 1944,
the Vieux Pont has been carefully restored. It is
backed by brightly painted houses with cluttered
balconies and nineteenth-century *trompe-l'œil*
decorations. Coupled with the magnificent mountain
backdrop, it is one of the best views in this appealing
little town.

*High above Sospel, cupped snugly in its fertile
hollow, lies the Saint-Roch fort, part of the
ill-fated Maginot Line (opposite). Sospel is a quiet place,
somewhere to appreciate detail: a carving on a house in
the Rue de la République (above); sunlight on the south
side of Saint-Michel (above right); the arcades of the Rue
de la République, the old salt road of Saint-Nicolas
(right); and houses clinging crazily to the hillside above
the town (overleaf).*

# *Vence*

## ALPES-MARITIMES

A CURVED, MEDIEVAL WALL once enclosed Vence, protecting it from invasion by its enemies. The town is still embraced by its remains, which serve today as shelter from intrusion by modern life. Cars are excluded from the old town, a patchwork of tiny squares linked by narrow, winding streets which echo to the sound of footsteps and voices.

Vence's old cathedral stands on the Place Clemenceau, the busy heart of the old town. It is so small, however, that standing amid the market stalls and bustling crowds, you could be forgiven for overlooking it altogether. Like Vence itself, the building is a magnificent amalgam of different architectural periods. Its site was once occupied by a temple dedicated to Mars and Cybele, and classical inscriptions are set into its pretty Baroque façade. In the fourth century, when Christianity took hold and Vence became a bishopric, a church was built in place of the temple. St. Veranus was one of Vence's earliest bishops. Canonized immediately after his death in 481

*The line of the medieval town wall is clearly visible from a distance* (left), *although the ramparts have long been superseded by houses. Brightly coloured daisies have enlivened a grassy slope beneath the Ermitage Notre-Dame-de-Vie* (above), *not far from Vence.*

159

*T*he narrow façade of Vence's former cathedral (opposite) is a surprisingly modest presence on the Place Clemenceau. In the cathedral's south chapel (left) stands a fifth-century sarcophagus, said to be the tomb of St. Veranus; other early carvings there include this figure of a Roman tribune (below).

by popular request, he was loved by the people as much for his spiritual work as for his involvement in the defence of the city against invasion by the Visigoths and Ostrogoths. A beautifully carved fifth-century sarcophagus that once contained the saint's body stands in the south chapel nearest to the high altar.

It was not until after Veranus' death that the Saracens succeeded in storming the city and razing the cathedral to the ground. The heart of the existing building, which has been enlarged and altered constantly over the centuries, is pure Romanesque. Behind the tiny façade it opens out into a substantial nave with four aisles. Fragments of every preceding

structure have been amalgamated into the new building. Roman inscriptions can be found in the exterior walls and the porch, and in the chapel of the Holy Sacrament there are fragments of exquisite Carolingian carving depicting grapes, birds, flowers and leaves in knotted roundels. The magnificent Gothic choir stalls date from a much later period in the history of the cathedral. They were the work of Jacques Bellot, a fifteenth-century sculptor from Grasse. Marc Chagall's mosaic of Moses was installed in the baptistery in 1979.

The fragments of antique masonry and engraved plaques incorporated into the streets and buildings all over Vence are particularly noticeable in the Place du

*The Rue du Portail-Levis* (left) *is typical of old Vence; it leads from the centre to one of the town gates, which was formerly defended by a drawbridge and could be emphatically closed with a portcullis. The town is full of attractive, secretive doorways, like the entrance to the Hôtel-Dieu* (opposite) *and the elaborate doorway of a house on the Place du Frêne* (below).

Peyra - once the site of the forum. The square is on the edge of the old town, just inside the Porte du Peyra, one of five gates that pierce the medieval wall. It is overlooked by the thirteenth-century tower of a castle that belonged to the Villeneuve family who ruled Vence from the tenth century until they were ousted during the Revolution.

The family reached the height of its power under Romée Villeneuve, an influential figure in the court of Raymond Bérenger IV, Count of Provence. It is said that the brilliant marriages made by Bérenger's daughters were negotiated by Villeneuve. Despite their father's inability to offer tempting dowries, all four

girls married kings. Marguerite, the eldest, married Louis IX of France, Eleanor married Henry III and became Queen of England, Sancia married Henry's brother, Richard, Duke of Cornwall, who became King of the Romans, and finally, Beatrice married Charles of Anjou and became Queen of the Two Sicilies.

D. H. Lawrence was one among many twentieth-century artists and writers who spent the end of their lives in Vence, drawn to it by the quality of the light and the gentle climate of the Riviera. The charming English library and the Anglican church reflect this tradition. Henri Matisse also lived in the town. In 1941

he began work on the Chapelle du Rosaire which stands on the hillside above Vence. Everything in it was made to his design, from the simple line-drawings on the walls to the last detail of the vestments and candlesticks. The chapel was his gift to the Dominican convent where he had been nursed back to health after a long illness during the war. In a letter to the local bishop, Matisse said, 'This work has taken me four years of exclusive and assiduous work and it represents the result of my entire active life. I consider it, in spite of its imperfections, to be my masterpiece'.

*The fresh local produce* (above *and* left), *so plentiful in the local market, no doubt finds its way to the tables of local restaurants* (opposite).

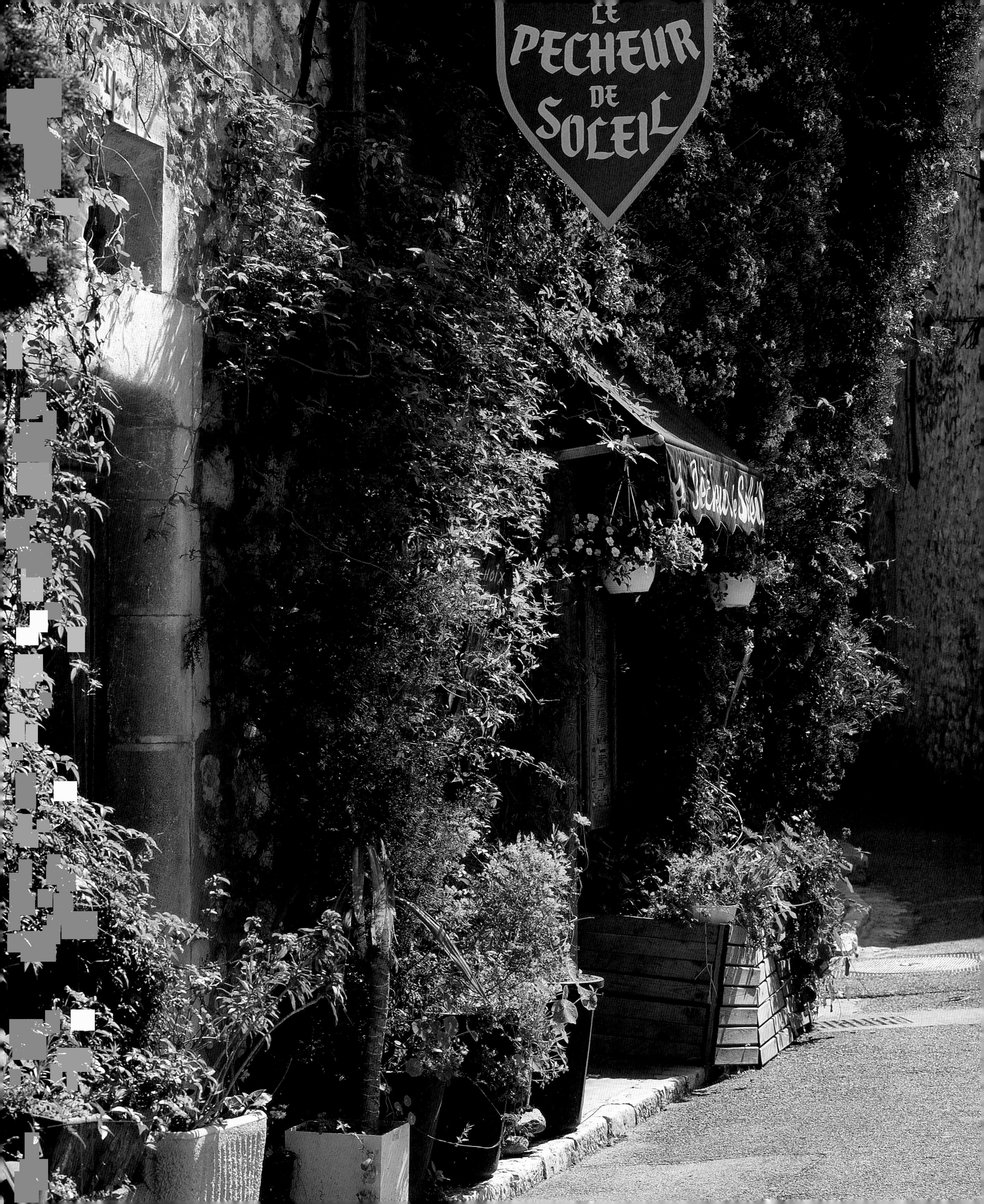
LE
PECHEUR
DE
SOLEIL

# Barcelonnette

### ALPES-DE-HAUTE-PROVENCE

A SUNNY, WELCOMING RESORT TOWN, Barcelonnette basks in the heart of the Ubaye valley. Beloved of walkers in summer and ski parties in winter, its main streets yield dramatic views of snowy mountain peaks in all directions. Even in midsummer, the heat is leavened by a cool breeze.

The early history of Barcelonnette is well documented. It was founded in 1231 as a frontier town, a bastion on the rugged, northernmost fringe of Raymond Bérenger IV's kingdom. The foundation charter, caked in sealing wax and bearing Bérenger's signature, is displayed in the local museum. He named the new settlement Barcelone, a reference to his own title. As grandson of Alfonso I of Aragon, Raymond was Count of Barcelona as well as Provence. By strange coincidence, the Hispanic ring of the name became doubly appropriate in the nineteenth century, in a way that Bérenger could never have imagined. The harsh conditions of life in the mountain valley prompted a wave of emigration from Barcelonnette to Mexico. Successful emigrants, returning wealthy and triumphant to their birthplace, built themselves the

*T he orderly streets and roofs of the town* (left) *look towards the picturesquely named mountains of the Pain de Sucre and the Chapeau de Gendarme to the south. Its neat town-hall* (above) *was built with funds subscribed by returning emigrants.*

Mexican-style villas that give a unique and eccentric character to the town. The Mexican atmosphere is accentuated by the ponchos hanging in shop windows on the Place Manuel, the taco restaurants and the courses in Mexican culture at the Maison du Mexique.

Bérenger intended Barcelone to stand sentinel over his land. Instead, it proved a provocation and a temptation to all comers. Its inhabitants suffered frequent and sustained attacks. By 1388 the town had fallen to the Counts of Savoy who held on to it, nominally at least, until 1713. Throughout this period Barcelone was repeatedly attacked and numerous religious and political battles were fought over the Ubaye valley.

In 1713 the Counts of Savoy were persuaded to exchange the town, now known as Barcelonnette, for part of the Dauphiné under the Treaty of Utrecht. This exchange, which was negotiated for Louis XIV by Marshal Berwick, brought the Ubaye into the kingdom of France. A statue of Berwick, a hero in the town, stands on the Place Manuel, a sunny square that marks the bustling centre of the town. Although born and educated in France, Berwick was the illegitimate son of King James II and Arabella Churchill. An acknowledged expert in alpine warfare, he invented a small cannon that could be transported on the back of a mule.

*The Hispanic connections of the town are displayed everywhere: the main street* (opposite) *is named the Rue Manuel; the architecture of local houses is often distinctly Spanish colonial* (below). *The Villa Sapinière* (right), *another summer house built by a returning emigrant, now houses a local history museum. The alpine setting of the town is indicated by the overshot roof of the Hôtel du Cheval Blanc* (above right).

Most of Barcelonnette's medieval quarter was burnt down at the beginning of the seventeenth century when French troops stormed the town bearing flaming torches. A Dominican convent, founded in 1316, once stood on the Place Manuel. Partly destroyed in the sixteenth century, it was finally demolished during the Revolution. All that remains is the fifteenth-century *clocher* that towers over the brightly painted buildings and café tables lining the main square. The comfortable buildings of the main street, with their overhanging roofs, date mainly from the eighteenth and nineteenth centuries.

The most conspicuous houses in Barcelonnette are large nineteenth- and early twentieth-century summer villas built by the emigrants returning from Mexico. They were not designed to be inhabited during the harsh, Ubaye winters, when their owners retreated to the Riviera. Fifty houses were built in all, on the outskirts of Barcelonnette and the road to Jausiers, but for many of them winter is now perpetual. Vast and alien against the mountain backdrop, they stand in a sea of long grass that waves over the ruin of their gardens. The Villa Sapinière, on the other hand, is in a fine state of repair and houses a magnificent local history museum. Upstairs, part of the original Hispanic interior is preserved.

*E nticing alpine meadows lie above the Lac du Serre Ponçon (left), a short expedition from Barcelonnette. Sadly, the surrounds of the town are also the setting for a number of abandoned houses originally built by emigrants returning from Mexico (above).*

*The tiny church of Saint-Pons (below), just outside Barcelonnette, once formed part of a Benedictine monastery; on its west door (left) a twelfth-century frieze shows souls flying heavenwards on the Day of Judgement. On the fifteenth-century south door to the cemetery there is a representation of the Crucifixion (far left). The centre of the town is dominated by the twelfth-century bell-tower of Saint-Pierre (opposite).*

Overleaf
*Close to Barcelonnette, the valley of the river Ubaye provides a dramatic setting for an isolated church.*

# Digne-les-Bains

## ALPES-DE-HAUTE-PROVENCE

THE POSITION OF THIS QUIET TOWN between the rocky bed of the Bléone and the foothills of the southern Alps could not be more spectacular. A centre of population ever since the Romans discovered a hot spring pouring from the Falaise Saint-Pancrace, east of the town, Digne's modern hotels now cater for visitors seeking relief from rheumatism.

Le Bourg, now a suburb of Digne, was once the centre of the Roman settlement. The town's former cathedral, Notre-Dame-du-Bourg, is an impressive Romanesque structure built from ochre-coloured limestone. The capitals of Roman pillars flank a handsome portal in the twelfth-century façade. Almost 800 years of alpine weather have virtually obliterated the features of the lions that stand sentinel on either side of the entrance. They would originally have supported the pillars of a wooden porch that sheltered the cathedral door. A new porch has recently been made, but it is adequately supported by the original stone corbels in the façade.

The cathedral's interior is thought to be slightly earlier than the façade. The Romanesque nave is bounded by blind arcading on either side. There are frescoes dating from the fourteenth, fifteenth and sixteenth centuries which show the Last Judgement and the cardinal vices and virtues. The white marble altar is thought to be Merovingian. During the Wars of Religion, Notre-Dame-du-Bourg was the site of an atrocity that has left an indelible mark on its structure. The Catholic population of the town was driven into the cathedral in 1591 by Protestant troops who then turned guns on their captives and massacred them. Most of the pillars in the nave have been replaced over the centuries, but the third one on the left is original. Its deep scars serve as a reminder of the cruelty inflicted in the name of religion. The massacre left the cathedral so badly damaged that its status was transferred to another church. As a result, Notre-Dame-du-Bourg has been preserved, virtually unaltered, since the sixteenth century.

*The town lies in the foothills of the southern Alps beneath rocky outcrops which resemble the spines of giant dinosaurs.*

*This magnificent twelfth-century portal of Notre-Dame-du-Bourg (far left) is one of several outstanding features of the town's former cathedral. Secular Digne is elegantly laid out with a variety of fountains (left and opposite) and a centre in the tree-lined Place Général de Gaulle (below).*

Digne's new church of Saint-Jérôme was built between 1490 and 1500. The centre of activity in Digne had long moved to the west by this time, away from Le Bourg. The new houses that had accumulated in the protective shadow of the castle on the steep hill of Saint-Charles now formed the hub of the town. As a result, the cathedral was no longer at the centre of the community that it served. Antoine Guiramand, Bishop of Digne from 1479 to 1513, commissioned the new church on a site close to the castle. He entrusted the work to Antoine Brolhon, a master mason from the alpine town of Barcelonnette. Saint-Jérôme stands at the top of the old town, flanked by a square *clocher* with an elaborate wrought-iron bell-cage. From the steps in front of it there is a spectacular view across the mighty rocks of the Vallon des Eaux-Chaudes, where the Rocher de Neuf-Heures rises like the back of a monstrous lizard.

*The elaborate bell-cage of the church of Saint-Jérôme towers above the roofs of the town* (below). *From its steps a magnificent panorama* (right) *stretches from the Rocher de Neuf-Heures to the Saint-Pancrace outcrop with the Barre des Dourbes in the background.*

# Forcalquier

## ALPES-DE-HAUTE-PROVENCE

FORCALQUIER IS ALWAYS BUSY ON MARKET-DAY. Stalls are set out on the Place du Bourguet and the bars and restaurants lining the square are full. At first glance it looks like a ordinary country town, but if you turn your back on the bustle of the market and walk into the old town, the streets have a grandeur that suggests a more opulent past. The houses have fine windows and elaborate barrel arches over their doors. The carved flowers, animals and arabesques are gradually crumbling away and time has blackened the limestone, which must once have been a dazzling white. Anyone who takes pleasure in faded grandeur should visit Forcalquier, for it is everywhere in these dark streets.

The beautiful houses scattered along the Rue du Collège and the Grande Rue were built between the fifteenth and seventeenth centuries, but Forcalquier's glory days began much earlier. Until the thirteenth century it was a small, independent state, but in 1209 its power and importance were increased beyond

*S*een from the north, Forcalquier clusters around the rock that was once the site of its castle (left), *and is now topped by the chapel of Notre-Dame-de-Provence* (above), *built in 1875.*

183

*Forcalquier is a town of quiet corners (opposite)* and *sometimes startling architectural detail, like this spiral staircase in the Place du Palais (above) and the ribald carvings on the pyramid fountain in the Place Saint-Michel (right centre). Among many fine doorways to the town's grander houses are these in the Rue Marius Debout (top) and the Place Saint-Michel (right below).*

measure by the marriage of Gersende de Sabran, Countess of Forcalquier, to Alphonse II, Count of Provence. For the next 200 years their descendants ruled Provence.

United with Provence, Forcalquier became capital of upper Provence, a wild, mountainous land stretching up the river Durance as far as Gap. The town threw off obscurity and its name became known throughout Europe as a centre of political and economic power. In the thirteenth century Raymond Bérenger IV strengthened its political position further through the marriages of his daughters.

Forcalquier retained its independence until 1481, when Provence became a part of the kingdom of France. At the height of its power, its court was second only in importance to that of Aix-en-Provence. Artists came to the town to seek the patronage of the Counts of Provence and it is said that Sordello, the famous troubadour, came to sing at the court.

*In spite of its compact form and relatively small size, Forcalquier offers an amazing variety of sights and settings: afternoon siesta in the Rue Chauran* (left)*; the labyrinthine nineteenth-century cemetery* (below)*, a listed site; and the nineteenth-century chapel of Notre-Dame-de-Provence* (opposite) *above the remains of the old castle.*

Sainte-Marie, Forcalquier's first church, was built in the twelfth century, just below the castle mound. In the early thirteenth century a new church was built which became a co-cathedral for the bishopric of Sisteron. Notre-Dame-du-Marché or du-Bourguet stands on the edge of the market square. The building has a plain, elegant façade with a fine Gothic doorway and a magnificent rose-window above it. Inside, the austere simplicity of the nave with its broken barrel-vaulting is typical of Provençal Romanesque. The two chapels that were added to the building slightly later are said to be the earliest examples of the Gothic style in Provence. There have been many subsequent additions to the cathedral, including the sixteenth-century bell-tower, but the severe simplicity of the interior is unharmed.

Among the other important buildings in the town was the Couvent des Cordeliers, or Franciscan convent. The Franciscans were known as Cordeliers because of the *cordes*, ropes, tied around their waists.

The convent was built on land given to the Franciscans by Raymond Bérenger IV in 1236, and it is one of the earliest Franciscan buildings in France. The pyramid fountain of Saint-Michel stands in a narrow square of the same name. It was built in 1512, when the Cordeliers brought a supply of fresh water to Forcalquier. The base, with its ribald carvings, is the only original part of the structure.

Inevitably, Forcalquier's wealth made it a target for attack. The castle, built on the summit of the hill by Raymond Bérenger, could not protect the town in 1380 from the repeated attacks of Raymond-Louis de Turenne of Les Baux. Famous for his cruelty, Turenne is said to have delighted in forcing his victims to jump off the castle walls, laughing at their fear. The real decline of the town began in the sixteenth century when it was devastated by the plague and the assaults of both Catholics and Protestants during the Wars of Religion. In 1601 its fate was sealed when the castle was pulled down by Henri IV. A few foundation stones are all that remain of the building on the citadel above the town. In 1875 the chapel of Notre-Dame-de-Provence was built on the site.

*The range of shops along the Rempart de Berluc-Perussis (left) and in the Place Vieille (above) reflects another side of Forcalquier – that of the vibrant market town.*

# Sisteron

ALPES-DE-HAUTE-PROVENCE

To describe Sisteron's setting as 'dramatic' would be sadly inadequate. The little town, with its monstrous fortress, is built in the only pass through the mountain barrier that separates Provence from the Dauphiné. It is bounded to the east by the river Durance and the massive, fractured face of the Rocher de la Baume. On its west side the town is dwarfed by the towering wall of the Montagne de l'Ubac. Despite overbearing surroundings and a history forged by warfare, modern Sisteron is a light-hearted place. Each week a market fills the Place de l'Horloge. A brass band playing beneath the clock-tower makes shopping a festive affair, and the local goats' cheeses are unrivalled.

Sisteron occupies a position of enormous strategic importance, and there has always been a fortress on the site. First the Ligurians and then the Celts built fortified bastions to guard the passage that the river Durance makes through the mountains. They were expelled by the Romans, who built a fort on the site. During the Middle Ages Sisteron stood on the northern frontier of the kingdom ruled by the Counts of Forcalquier and Provence. The eleventh-century citadel successfully repelled invasions from Savoy and the Dauphiné, but in 1481 the *comté* was finally absorbed into the kingdom of France.

The mountainous landscape does nothing to diminish the impact of the citadel that overshadows

*T*he belfry of the cathedral of Notre-Dame-des-Pommiers (above) rises clearly above the roofs of the town, strung out along the banks of the Durance (right).

Sisteron today. The keep and watch-tower date from the twelfth century, but the rest of the structure, with towering battlements and vertiginous views, was built by successive generations, responding to the ever more sophisticated technology of warfare. At the tail-end of the seventeenth century a massive programme of rebuilding was planned in response to the Duke of Savoy's invasion of the upper valley of the Durance. Vauban, Louis XIV's military engineer, was commissioned to design new defences in 1692. He drew up a vast plan that encompassed both the fortress and the town. In the event, the funding of the project proved so precarious that only a powder store and a well were built. Vauban's plans were brought out once again in 1842, the beginning of another phase of modernization. Work continued until 1860, and focused on increasing the height of the ramparts. An underground staircase was also built, linking the fortress to the north gate of the town.

For over 600 years Sisteron's fortress survived intact, strong enough to withstand even the ferocity of late-nineteenth-century warfare. It was not until the night of 15 August 1944 that it finally collapsed, when a squadron of American bombers, ordered to destroy the bridge over the river Buech, missed their target, unloading their cargo on the citadel and on the old town below it. (Continued on p.198)

*The view across the river Durance from the west reveals the rugged pinnacle of the Montagne de la Beaume (left). As with all Provençal towns, a dramatic setting is often the backdrop to traditional detail: a faded sign beneath the Couvert de Font Chaud (above). In Sisteron's case, the setting also includes one of the great river arteries of Provence – the Durance (overleaf).*

Complete rebuilding has denied the fortress any of the softening effects of age.

Sisteron lay on the route of Napoleon's glorious return from Elba to Paris and its fortress barred the sole route through the mountains. Despite Napoleon's forebodings, the advance party returned on 4 March 1815 with news that the fortress was deserted and stripped of its munitions. There were no cheering crowds to greet him, but Napoleon passed unhindered.

After the grim expanses of the fortress, it is a relief to go down through the bustling market in the Place de l'Horloge and into the narrow, crowded streets of the old town. Lying between the Rue Droite and the Durance, this is a web of tiny, vaulted passageways, known in local dialect as *andrônes*, running between thirteenth-century buildings. The cathedral of Notre-Dame-des-Pommiers stands outside the old town, close to four fourteenth-century towers that once formed part of the town's fortifications. Its name is in fact derived from the Latin *ponemurum*, an open space behind the city wall. Built between 1160 and 1220, it is considered one of the finest examples of Provençal Romanesque. A fantastic bestiary forms the frieze above the doorway. One of the largest churches in the area, it has a towering nave ending in an octagonal cupola. Over the altar a painting by Nicolas Mignard, brother of Pierre Mignard, *premier peintre* to Louis XIV, depicts angels playing their harps for the Holy Family.

*The narrow streets and crowded houses of the town are never very far from the barren rock faces that dominate it* (preceding pages *and* above). *High above is the citadel* (right) *that proved indestructible for 600 years.*

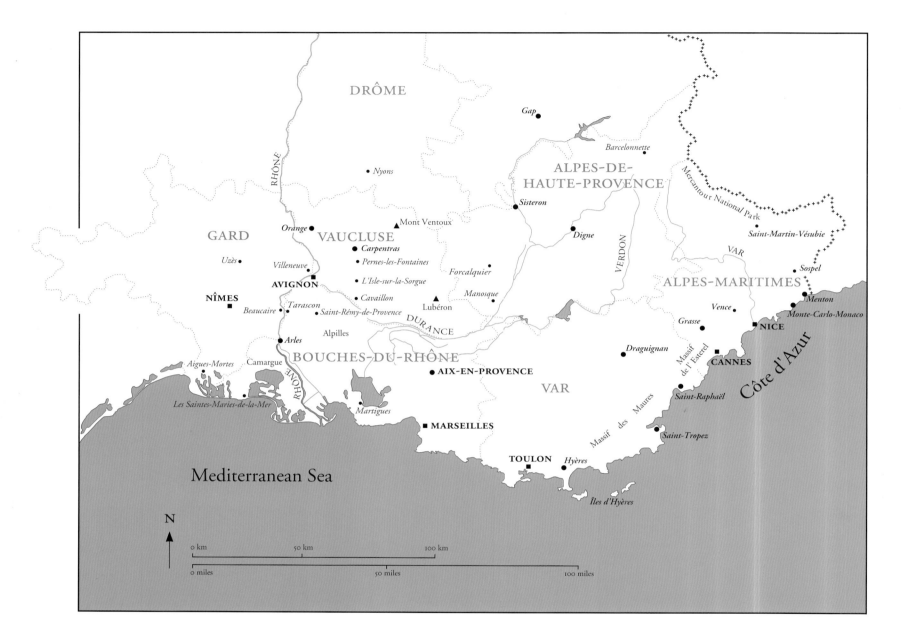

DRÔME

Gap

Barcelonnette

Nyons

ALPES-DE-
HAUTE-PROVENCE

Mercantour National Park

RHÔNE

Sisteron

GARD

Orange

VAUCLUSE

Mont Ventoux

Digne

VERDON

VAR

Saint-Martin-Vésubie

Uzès

Carpentras

Sospel

Villeneuve

Pernes-les-Fontaines

Forcalquier

ALPES-MARITIMES

AVIGNON

L'Isle-sur-la-Sorgue

Manosque

Menton

NÎMES

Cavaillon

Lubéron

Vence

Monte-Carlo-Monaco

Beaucaire

Tarascon

Saint-Rémy-de-Provence

DURANCE

Grasse

NICE

Arles

Alpilles

Draguignan

Massif
de l'Esterel

CANNES

Aigues-Mortes

Camargue

BOUCHES-DU-RHÔNE

Côte d'Azur

AIX-EN-PROVENCE

RHÔNE

VAR

Saint-Raphaël

Les Saintes-Maries-de-la-Mer

Martigues

MARSEILLES

Massif    des    Maures

Saint-Tropez

TOULON

Hyères

Mediterranean Sea

Îles d'Hyères

N

0 km        50 km        100 km

0 miles                50 miles                100 miles

# A Travellers' Guide

While every effort has been made to ensure that the information given in the following entries is correct, the author and the publisher cannot be held responsible for any inadvertent inaccuracies. Opening dates and times of local attractions change seasonally and sometimes alter from year to year; it is always advisable to check with the venue or the nearest tourist information office in advance. The lists of hotels and restaurants are very much those of the personal choice of the author and photographer.

## FRENCH TOURIST BOARDS

179 Piccadilly, London W1
tel. (0891) 244123.

38 Lower Abbey Street, Dublin 1
tel. (1) 703 4046.

444 Madison Avenue, New York, NY 10022
tel. (212) 838 7800.

9454 Wilshire Boulevard, Suite 715, Beverley Hills, Los Angeles, CA 90212
tel. (310) 271 2693.

30 St. Patrick's Street, Suite 700, Toronto, ONT M5T 3A3
tel. (416) 593 4723.

## GARD & BOUCHES-DU-RHÔNE

### Aigues-Mortes

*Sights & Events*
*Market day*; Wednesdays & Sundays a.m.
*Fête de Saint-Louis* (historic pageant with traditionally-dressed locals); late August.
*Tour de Constance and the town walls*; open May to September 9.30–19.00, June to August 9.30–20.00, October to April 10.00–17.00.
*Chapelle des Pénitents Gris*; guided tours Mondays, Wednesdays and Fridays 10.00–11.30.

*Where to stay*
HÔTEL LES REMPARTS, 6 place Anatole France;
tel. (0466) 538277.
HÔTEL LES ARCADES, 23 boulevard Gambetta;
tel. (0466) 538113.
HÔTEL VICTORIA, place Anatole France;
tel. (0466) 511420.

*Where to eat*
RESTAURANT ABACA, 424 route d'Arles;
tel. (0466) 537796.
CAFÉ DU COMMERCE, 11 place Saint-Louis;
tel. (0466) 537171.

*Information*
Porte de la Gardette, 30220 Aigues-Mortes;
tel. (0466) 537300.
www.ot-aiguesmortes.fr

### Arles

*Sights & Events*
*Market day*; Saturdays & Wednesdays; bric-à-brac on first Wednesday of the month.
*Feria Pascale* (Easter festival).
*Rencontres Internationales de la Photographie*; Europe's principal festival of photography, July.
*Fêtes d'Arles*; various events, including processions and bullfights, June/July.
*Les Arènes* (the Roman arena) & *Les Alyscamps* (the Roman necropolis); open daily, times vary.

*Where to stay*
GRAND HÔTEL NORD PINUS, 14 place du Forum;
tel. (0490) 934444.
HÔTEL LE FORUM, 10 place du Forum;
tel. (0490) 934895.
HÔTEL LE CLOÎTRE, 16 rue du Cloître;
tel. (0490) 962950.

*Where to eat*
RESTAURANT LOU MARQUÈS, 9 boulevard des Lices;
tel. (0490) 525252.
RESTAURANT LA GUEULE DU LOUP, 39 rue des Arènes;
tel. (0490) 969669.
RESTAURANT PLEIN SUD, 6 rue de la Rotonde; tel.
(0490) 969476.

*Information*
Boulevard des Lices, 13200 Arles; tel. (0490) 184120.
www.ville-arles.fr

### Saint-Rémy-de-Provence

*Sights & Events*
*Market day*; Wednesdays.
*Fête de la Transhumance* (procession of shepherds and their flocks through the town); Whit Monday.
*Feria* (festival); mid-August.
*Glanum* (Roman town); open April to September 9.00–19.00, October to March 9.00–12.00, 14.00–17.00.

*The cloisters of Saint-Paul-de-Mausole, Saint-Rémy-de-Provence.*

*Les Antiques* (Roman triumphal arch & mausoleum); open all year.
*Saint-Paul-de-Mausole*; open Tuesday to Saturday, May to October 9.00–19.00, November to April 9.00–17.30.
*Le Mas de la Pyramide* (cave dwelling); open in summer 9.00–12.00, 14.00–19.00, in winter 9.00–12.00.
*La Musée des Alpilles*; open July/August 10.00–12.00, 14.00–19.00, March to October 10.00–12.00, 14.00–18.00.

### Where to stay
HÔTEL LES ANTIQUES, 15 avenue Pasteur; tel. (0490) 920302.
HÔTEL LE CASTELET DES ALPILLES, 6 place Mireille; tel. (0490) 920721.
HÔTEL LE SOLEIL, 35 avenue Pasteur; tel. (0490) 920063.

### Where to eat
RESTAURANT LA GOUSSE D'AIL, 25 rue Carnot; tel. (0490) 921687.
RESTAURANT LA MAISON JAUNE, 15 rue Carnot; tel. (0490) 925614.
RESTAURANT LE BISTROT DES ALPILLES, 15 boulevard Mirabeau; tel. (0490) 920917.

### Information
Place Jean-Jaurès, 13210 Saint-Rémy-de-Provence; fax (0490) 923852.
www.saintremy-de-provence.com

## Tarascon & Beaucaire

### Sights & Events
*Market day*; Tuesdays (Tarascon), Thursdays & Sundays (Beaucaire).
*Les Estivales* (traditional festival with bullfighting in Beaucaire); last week in July.
*Les Beaux Quais du Vendredi* (evening markets & performances around the marina in Beaucaire); July & August.
*Fête du Tarasque* (procession with the Tarasque monster and Daudet's famous character Tartarin, in Tarascon); last weekend in June.
*Château de Tarascon*; open April to September 9.00–19.00, October to March 9.00–12.00, 14.00–17.00; closed Tuesdays.
*Château de Beaucaire* (& demonstrations of falconry); open April to October 10.00–12.00, 14.15–18.45, November to March 10.15–12.00, 14.00–17.15; closed Tuesdays.

### Where to stay
HÔTEL DE PROVENCE, 7 boulevard Victor-Hugo, Tarascon; tel. (0490) 435813.
HÔTEL LES ÉCHEVINS, 26 boulevard Itam, Tarascon; tel. (0490) 910170.

### Where to eat
BISTROT DES ANGES, place du Marché, Tarascon.

### Information
59 rue des Halles, Tarascon; tel. (0490) 910352.

## Uzès

### Sights & Events
*Market day*; Wednesdays & Saturdays.
*Nuits musicales d'Uzès*; (Early Music festival); late July.
*La Duché* (ducal palace); guided tours daily, July to August 10.00–18.30, September to June 10.00–12.00, 14.00–18.00.

### Where to stay
HÔTEL D'ENTRAIGUES, place de l'Évêché; tel. (0466) 223268.
HÔTEL SAINT-GENIÈS, route de Barjac, Saint-Ambroix; tel. (0466) 222999.
HÔTEL LA TAVERNE, rue Xavier Sigalon; tel. (0466) 221310.

### Where to eat
RESTAURANT LE JARDIN DES OLIVIERS, chemin du Pont Romain; tel. (0466) 226084.
RESTAURANT L'ÉCRIN DES SAVEURS, 3 boulevard Charles Gide; tel. (0466) 223521.
RESTAURANT ZANELLI, 3 place Nicolas Froment; tel. (0466) 030193.

### Information
Place Albert 1er, 30703 Uzès; tel. (0466) 226888.
www.ville-uzes.fr

## Villeneuve-lès-Avignon

**Sights & Events**
*Market day*; Thursdays.
*Fête de Saint-Marc* (festival & procession of the patron saint of wine-growers); early May.
*Chartreuse du Val de Bénédiction* (monastery); open April to September 9.00–18.30, October to March 9.30–17.30.
*Fort Saint-André*; open April to September 10.00–12.30, 14.00–18.00, October to March 10.00–12.00, 14.00–17.00.
*Musée Municipal Pierre-de-Luxembourg*; open April to September 10.00–12.30, 15.00–19.00, October to March 10.00–12.00, 14.00–17.00; closed Mondays.
*Notre-Dame* (church); open April to September 10.00–12.30, 3.00–7.00, October to March 10.00–12.00, 2.00–5.30; closed Mondays.

**Where to stay**
HÔTEL LE PRIEURÉ, 7 place du Chapitre; tel. (0490) 159015.
HÔTEL LA MAGNANERAIE, 37 rue Camp de Bataille; tel. (0490) 251111.
HÔTEL L'ATELIER, 5 rue de la Foire; tel. (0490) 250184.

**Where to eat**
RESTAURANT AUBERTIN, 1 rue de l'Hôpital; tel. (0490) 259484.
RESTAURANT LE POTAGER DE LA TOUR, 35 avenue Gabriel Péri; tel. (0490) 253144.
RESTAURANT LES JARDINS DE LA LIVRÉE, 4 bis rue Camp de Bataille; tel. (0490) 260505.

**Information**
1 place Charles-David, 30400 Villeneuve-lès-Avignon; tel. (0490) 256133.
www.villeneuve-lez-avignon.com

*P*rovençal textiles in the weekly market at Villeneuve-lès-Avignon.

# VAR & VAUCLUSE

## Carpentras

**Sights & Events**
*Market day*; Tuesdays & Fridays; truffle market every Friday from 27 November to March.
*Corso de Nuit* (procession of illuminated floats); mid-July.
*Saint-Siffrein* (cathedral); open summer 10.00–12.00, 14.00–18.00, winter 10.00–12.00, 14.00–16.00.
*Hôtel-Dieu* (perfectly preserved eighteenth-century pharmacy); open Monday, Wednesday & Thursday on request, 9.00–11.30.
*Synagogue* (fourteenth-century); open Monday to Friday 10.00–12.00, 15.00–17.00.

**Where to stay**
HÔTEL LE COQ HARDI, 36 place de la Marotte; tel. (0490) 630035.
HÔTEL LE FIACRE, 153 rue Vigne; tel. (0490) 630315.
HÔTEL FORUM, 24 rue du Forum; tel. (0490) 605700.

**Where to eat**
RESTAURANT ATELIER DE PIERRE, 30 place de l'Horloge; tel. (0490) 607500.
RESTAURANT VERT GALANT, 12 rue de Clapiès; tel. (0490) 671550.

**Information**
170 allée Jean-Jaurès, 84200 Carpentras; tel. (0490) 630078.
www.tourisme.fr/carpentras

## Hyères

**Sights & Events**
*Market day*; Tuesdays, Thursdays & Saturdays.
*Sailing week*; April.

**Where to stay**
HÔTEL CASINO DES PALMIERS, 1 rue Ambroise Thomas; tel. (0494) 128080.
HÔTEL LE PORTALET, 4 rue de Limans; tel. (0494) 653940.
HÔTEL DU SOLEIL, rue du Rempart; tel. (0494) 651626.

**Where to eat**
RESTAURANT LE HAUT DU PAVÉ, place Massillon; tel. (0494) 352098.
RESTAURANT LES JARDINS DE BACCHUS, 32 avenue Gambetta; tel. (0494) 657763.

**Information**
3 avenue Ambroise Thomas, 83400 Hyères; tel. (0494) 018450.
www.ot-hyeres.fr

## L'Isle-sur-la-Sorgue

**Sights & Events**
*Market day*; Thursdays & Sundays; largest antiques &

bric-à-brac market in Provence every Sunday.
*Marché flottant* (festival); first Sunday in August.
*Festival de la Sorgue* (music, theatre & dance); July.
*Notre-Dame-des-Anges* (church); open June to August
9.00–19.30, September to May 10.00–12.00,
15.00–18.00; closed Mondays.

### Where to stay
Hôtel Le Mas de Curé Bourse, route de Caumont-
sur-Durance; tel. (0490) 381658.
Hôtel Les Névons, chemin des Névons;
tel. (0490) 207200.
Hôtel Le Pescador, Partages-des-Eaux;
tel. (0490) 380969.

### Where to eat
Restaurant Le Mas de Curé Bourse (see hotel of
same name under *Where to stay* above).
Restaurant La Prévôté, 4 rue J.-J. Rousseau;
tel. (0490) 385729.

### Information
Place de l'Église; tel. (0490) 380478.
www.ot-islesurlasorgue.fr

## Nyons (Drôme)

### Sights & Events
*Market day*; Thursdays.
*Fête de l'Alicoque* (festival for the new olive oil); first
weekend in February.
*Corso Fleuri* (flower festival); Easter.

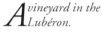

*A vineyard in the Lubéron.*

*Olive festival*; mid-July.
*Pont Roman* (medieval bridge).

### Where to stay
Hôtel La Caravelle, 8 rue des Antignans;
tel. (0475) 260744.
Hôtel Colombet, 53 place de la Libération;
tel. (0475) 260366.
Hôtel Les Oliviers, 2 rue André Escoffier;
tel. (0475) 261144.

### Where to eat
Restaurant Le Petit Caveau, 9 rue Victor Hugo;
tel. (0475) 262021.
Restaurant Le Resto des Arts, 13 rue des Déportés;
tel. (0475) 263149.
Restaurant La Picholine, promenade de la Perrière;
tel. (0475) 260621.

### Information
Place de la Libération, 26110 Nyons;
tel. (0475) 261035.
www.guideweb.com/nyons

## Pernes-les-Fontaines

### Sights & Events
*Market day*; Saturdays.
*Porte Notre-Dame* (picturesque sixteenth-century gate
and bridge).
*Tour Ferrande* (medieval tower with thirteenth-
century frescoes); guided tours by appointment with
the tourist information office.

### Where to stay
Hôtel La Margelle, place Aristide-Briand;
tel. (0490) 613036.

### Where to eat
Restaurant Au Fil du Temps, place L. Giraud;
tel. (0490) 664861.

### Information
Place Gabriel Moutte, 84210 Pernes-les-Fontaines;
tel. (0490) 613104.

# ALPES-DE-HAUTE-PROVENCE & ALPES-MARITIMES

## Grasse

### Sights & Events
*Market day*; daily flower & vegetable market;
Provençal market (local food & produce), first Saturday
of the month; fleamarket, second Saturday of the
month; book market, third Saturday of the month.
*Expo-Rose* (international rose festival); mid-May.
*Fête du Jasmin* (festival celebrating the jasmine
harvest); first week in August.
*Parfumerie Fragonard*; tel. (0493) 364465. *Parfumerie
Galimard*; tel. (0493) 092000. *Parfumerie Molinard*;

*I*n the Place aux Aires, Grasse.

*Festival de Musique de Chambre* (festival of chamber music); first fortnight in August.
*Saint-Michel* (church); open 10.00–12.00, 15.00–17.00.
*Cimetière du Vieux-Château* (cemetery).
*Hôtel de Ville* (Salle des Mariages decorated by Jean Cocteau); open Monday to Friday 8.30–12.30, 13.30–17.00.

### Where to stay
HÔTEL DES AMBASSADEURS, 3 rue Partouneaux; tel. (0493) 287575.
HÔTEL L'AIGLON, 7 avenue de la Madone; tel. (0493) 575555.
HÔTEL NAPOLÉON, 29 porte de France; tel. (0493) 358950.

### Where to eat
RESTAURANT LE LION D'OR, 7 rue des Marins; tel. (0493) 357467.
RESTAURANT LE DARKOUM, 23 rue Saint-Michel; tel. (0493) 354488.

### Information
8 avenue Boyer, 06506 Menton; tel. (0492) 417676.
www.villedementon.com

## Saint-Martin-Vésubie

### Sights & Events
*Fête du Pain* (bread festival); July.
*Notre-Dame de Fenestre*; mountain pilgrimage early July & late September.
*Chapelle des Pénitents Blancs*; tourist information office for opening hours.
*Chapelle de la Miséricorde*; tourist information office for opening hours.

### Where to stay
HÔTEL LA BONNE AUBERGE, allée de Verdun; tel. (0493) 032049.
HÔTEL LA CHÂTAIGNERAIE, allée de Verdun; tel. (0493) 032122.

### Where to eat
RESTAURANT LA TRAPPA, place du Marché; tel. (0493) 032150.
RESTAURANT LA BONNE AUBERGE (see hotel of same name under *Where to stay* above).

### Information
Place Félix Fauré, 06450 Saint-Martin-Vésubie; tel. (0493) 032128.

## Sospel

### Sights & Events
*Market day*; Thursdays & Sundays.
*Procession of the Penitents*; Holy Week.
*Fort Saint-Roch* (part of the Maginot line); guided tours daily except Mondays; open June to September 14.00–18.00, April, May & October, weekends & public holidays only, 14.00–18.00; closed November to March.

tel. (0493) 360162; all offer free guided tours daily except Sundays.

### Where to stay
HÔTEL BASTIDE SAINT-ANTOINE, 48 avenue Henri Dunant; tel. (0493) 709494.
HÔTEL VICTORIA, 7 avenue Riou Blanquet; tel. (0493) 403030.
HÔTEL DU PATTI, place du Patti; tel. (0493) 360100.

### Where to eat
RESTAURANT BASTIDE SAINT-ANTOINE (see hotel of same name under *Where to stay* above).
RESTAURANT AUBERGE DE L'ALAMBIC, 2 place de la Poissonnerie; tel. (0493) 364575.
RESTAURANT LE MOULIN DES PAROIRS, 2 avenue Jean XXIII; tel. (0493) 401040.

### Information
Palais des Congrès, 22 cours Honoré Cresp, 06130 Grasse; tel. (0493) 366666.
www.ville-grasse.fr

## Menton

### Sights & Events
*Market day*; daily covered market.
*Fête du Citron* (lemon festival); February.

*The fossilized shells of ammonites, near Digne-les-Bains.*

during school holidays daily 14.30–17.30; closed Sundays & Mondays.

### Where to stay
HÔTEL LA ROSERAIE, avenue H. Giraud; tel. (0493) 580220.
HÔTEL LE PROVENCE, 9 avenue M. Maurel; tel. (0493) 580421.
HÔTEL LA CLOSERIE DES GENÊTS, impasse M. Maurel; tel. (0493) 583325.

### Where to eat
RESTAURANT DOMAINE SAINT-MARTIN, avenue des Templiers; tel. (0493) 580202.
RESTAURANT LA CLOSERIE DES GENÊTS (see hotel of same name under *Where to stay* above).
RESTAURANT MAXIMIN, 686 chemin de la Gaude; tel. (0493) 589075.

### Information
8 place du Grand Jardin, Vence; tel. (0493) 580638.

## Barcelonnette

### Sights & Events
*Market day*; Wednesdays & Saturdays.
*Fête du Pain* (bread festival); 1 May.
*Corso Fleuri* (flower festival); 3 June.
*Les Journées du Mexique* (celebration of the town's Mexican links); 13–15 August.
*Musée de la Vallée*; open July to August 9.30–12.00, 14.30–19.00, June & September 15.00–19.00 (closed Sundays & Mondays); other months; Wednesdays, Thursdays & Saturdays 15.00–18.00.

### Where to stay
HÔTEL AZTECA, 3 rue François Arnaud; tel. (0492) 814636.
HÔTEL LE CHEVAL BLANC, 12 rue Grenette; tel. (0492) 810019.
HÔTEL L'AUPILLON, 9 avenue Ernest Pellotier; tel. (0492) 810109.

### Where to eat
RESTAURANT LA MANGEOIRE, place des Quatre-Vents; tel. (0492) 810161.
RESTAURANT LE TROUBADOUR, place Frédéric Mistral; tel. (0492) 812424.

### Information
Place Frédéric Mistral, 04400 Barcelonnette; tel. (0492) 810471.
www.barcelonnette.net

### Where to stay
HÔTEL-RESTAURANT DE FRANCE, 9 boulevard de Verdun; tel. (0493) 040001.
AUBERGE PROVENÇALE, route du Col de Castillor.; tel. (0493) 040031.

### Where to eat
RESTAURANT L'ESCARGOT D'OR, 3 rue de Verdun; tel. (0493) 040043.
HÔTEL RESTAURANT DES ÉTRANGERS, 7 boulevard de Verdun; tel. (0493) 040009.

### Information
Le Pont Vieux, 06380 Sospel; tel. (0493) 041580.

## Vence

### Sights & Events
*Market day*; Tuesdays & Fridays.
*Provençal folklore festival*; Easter Sunday & Monday.
*Classical & world music festival*; July to August.
*Chapelle du Rosaire* (decorated by Matisse); open Tuesdays & Thursdays 10.00–11.30, 14.30–17.30;

## Digne-les-Bains

### Sights & Events
*Corso de la Lavande*; first week in August.
*Les Journées Lavandes*; 23–27 August.
*Fondation Alexandra David-Neel* (fascinating collection of Tibetan artifacts collected over many years); free guided tours daily from 10.30.

World War II museum; open May to October, Wednesdays 14.00–17.00, July to August, daily 14.00–18.00.

**Where to stay**
HÔTEL DU GRAND PARIS, 19 boulevard Thiers; tel. (0492) 311115.
HÔTEL DE PROVENCE, 17 boulevard Thiers; tel. (0492) 313219.
HÔTEL DU PETIT SAINT-JEAN, 14 cours des Arès; tel. (0492) 313004.

**Where to eat**
RESTAURANT LE GRAND PARIS (see hotel of same name under **Where to stay** above).
RESTAURANT L'ORIGAN, 6 rue Pied de Ville; tel. (0492) 316213.
RESTAURANT LE BOURGOGNE, 3 avenue de Verdun; tel. (0492) 310019.

**Information**
Place du Tampinet, 04000 Digne-les-Bains; tel. (0492) 366262.
www.ot-dignelesbains.fr

## Forcalquier

**Sights & Events**
*Market day*; Mondays (fair on first Monday of the month).
*Craft fair*; late April and July & August.
*Couvent des Cordeliers*; guided tours May to October, Sundays & public holidays only, 14.00 & 16.30; July to September, Sundays & public holidays only, guided tours throughout the day.
*Terrasse Notre-Dame-de-Provence* (spectacular views from above the town).

*Traditional baking in Forcalquier.*

**Where to stay**
HOSTELLERIE DES DEUX LIONS, 11 place du Bourguet; tel. (0492) 752530.
GRAND HÔTEL, 10 boulevard Latourette; tel. (0492) 750035.
AUBERGE CHAREMBEAU, route de Niozelles; tel. (0492) 709170.

**Where to eat**
HOSTELLERIE DES DEUX LIONS (see under **Where to stay** above).
RESTAURANT LE LAPIN TANT PIS, place Vieille; tel. (0492) 753888.

**Information**
13 place du Bourguet, 04301 Forcalquier; tel. (0492) 751002.
www.forcalquier.com

## Sisteron

**Sights & Events**
*Market day*; Wednesdays & Saturdays (fair on second Saturday of the month).
*Nuits de la Citadelle* (dance & theatre in the castle); mid-July to mid-August.
*La Citadelle*; open May to October 9.00–18.30, June to July 9.00–19.30, November to April 9.00–17.30.

**Where to stay**
GRAND HÔTEL DU COURS, allée de Verdun; tel. (0492) 610451.
HÔTEL LE TIVOLI, 21 place René Cassin; tel. (0492) 611516.
HÔTEL LA CITADELLE, 126 rue Saunerie; tel. (0492) 611352.

**Where to eat**
RESTAURANT LES BECS FINS, rue Saunerie; tel. (0492) 611204.
RESTAURANT LE COURS, allée de Verdun; tel. (0492) 610050.

**Information**
*Hôtel de Ville*, 04202 Sisteron; tel. (0492) 611203.
www.sisteron.com

# Select Bibliography

BELLOC, Hilaire, *Hills and the Sea*, London, 1906
BENOÎT, F., *La Provence et Le Comtat Venaissin: Arts et Traditions Populaires*, Avignon, 1975
BENTLEY, James, *Provence and the Côte d'Azur*, London, 1992
BLUME, Mary, *Côte d'Azur: Inventing the French Riviera*, London, 1992
CÉZANNE, Paul, *Letters* (ed. John Rewald & Bruno Cassirer), London, 1941
CLAPHAM, A. W., *The Renaissance of Architecture and Stone Carving in Southern France in the 10th and 11th Centuries*, London, 1932
CONNOLLY, Cyril, *The Rock Pool*, Paris, 1936
DAUDET, Alphonse, *Lettres de Mon Moulin*, Paris, 1868
DAVID, Elizabeth, *French Provincial Cooking*, London, 1960
DURRELL, Lawrence, *Caesar's Vast Ghost (Aspects of Provence)*, London, 1990
FLOWER, John, *Provence*, London, 1987
FORD, Ford Madox, *Provence: From Minstrels to the Machine*, London, 1935
GIONO, J., *Provence Perdue*, Paris, 1967
JACOBS, Michael, *A Guide to Provence*, London, 1988
JACOBS, Michael, *The Most Beautiful Villages of Provence*, London, 1994
LONDON, Jack, *Troubadours and their World*, London, 1976
MARKHAM, Violet, *Romanesque France*, London, 1929
MISTRAL, Frédéric, *Memoirs of Mistral* (trans. Constance Elizabeth Maud), London, 1907
PAGAN, Francis, *Provence*, London, 1991
PAGNOL, Marcel, *La Gloire de Mon Père*, Paris, 1957
PAGNOL, Marcel, *Le Château de Ma Mère*, Paris, 1958
PAGNOL, Marcel, *Les Temps des Secrets*, Paris, 1960
POPE-HENNESSY, James, *Aspects of Provence*, London, 1952
RAISON, Laura, *The South of France, an Anthology*, London, 1985
SMOLLETT, Tobias, *Travels Through France and Italy*, London, 1766
WYLIE, L., *Village in the Vaucluse*, Cambridge (Mass.), 1977

# Author's and Photographer's Acknowledgments

We are especially grateful to the local tourist boards in Provence for their enthusiasm and helpfulness. We are particularly indebted to Isabelle des Aubrys of the tourist office in Sospel, to the director of tourism in Uzès and to Colette Giudicelli of the Mairie in Menton. Our thanks go also to Nadège Favergeon and the conservation department of the Musées du Gard for permission to photograph the *Couronnement de la Vierge* in Villeneuve-lès-Avignon, to M. Bellet, *administrateur-conservateur* in Aigues-Mortes, for permission to photograph the ramparts of the town, and to the Duc d'Uzès for permission to photograph the Duché d'Uzès. M. le Curé of Saint-Martin-Vésubie and Robert Benoît, verger of Saint-Siffrein in Carpentras, were only two of the many people who kindly displayed the treasures in their care. Finally, our thanks to Karen and Sam for getting us off to such a good start.